# Sprawl & Politics

SUNY series in Urban Public Policy

C. Theodore Koebe and Diane L. Zahm, editors

# Sprawl & Politics

*The Inside Story of
Smart Growth in Maryland*

John W. Frece

State University of New York Press

Published by
State University of New York Press, Albany

For information, contact State University of New York Press, Albany, NY
www.sunypress.edu

Production by Kelli W. LeRoux
Marketing by Michael Campochiaro


**Library of Congress Cataloging-in-Publication Data**

Frece, John W.
    Sprawl and politics : the inside story of smart growth in Maryland / John W.
Frece ; with a foreword by Gerrit-Jan Knaap.
        p. cm. — (SUNY series in urban public policy)
    Includes bibliographical references and index.
    ISBN-13: 978-0-7914-7411-2 (hardcover : alk. paper)
    ISBN-13: 978-0-7914-7412-9 (pbk. : alk. paper)    1. Land use—Maryland.
2. Sustainable development—Maryland.    3. City planning—Maryland.    I. Title.
HD211.M3F74 2008
338.9752—dc22

                                                                              2007035615

                                        10  9  8  7  6  5  4  3  2  1

*For Priscilla*

# Contents

# Illustrations

**Maps**

# Acknowledgments

This book grew out of plans to write a single chapter about the politics of Maryland's Smart Growth initiative within another, longer book about the program. But one chapter turned into two and two became four and soon it was a book by itself. This is because so much of what happened with Maryland's Smart Growth program—as with most government policy— was driven by politics: the political ambition of a governor and that of the legislators, county and municipal officials, environmental and business lobbyists, and others with whom that governor had no choice but to deal.

The idea to write about the politics of the Maryland program came from Dr. Gerrit-Jan Knaap, executive director of the National Center for Smart Growth Research and Education at the University of Maryland. The project began with financial support from the Lincoln Institute of Land Policy in Cambridge, Mass.

None of this, of course, could have been written had former Maryland governor Parris N. Glendening not put the author in the position to be part of the birth and evolution of the Maryland Smart Growth program. I will forever be indebted to him for the opportunities he provided me.

To recall what happened during those years, I called on a number of my former colleagues and longtime friends to give their perspective, including Jim Cohen, Grant Dehart, Ray Feldmann, John Griffin, Ron Kreitner, Steve Larsen, Jim Noonan, John Porcari, and Harriet Tregoning. Their cooperation was invaluable.

Thanks also for the support of Sandra A. Banisky, deputy managing editor of the *Baltimore Sun*, and *Sun* librarian Paul McCardell, who helped locate and make available photographs used in this book. My appreciation also is extended to Megan Rhodes at the Maryland Department of Planning for her help in providing updated versions of the "Red Tide" maps of Maryland.

Finally, I want to thank Dr. Michael Rinella, senior acquisitions editor at the State University of New York Press, for having the confidence to publish this book.

# Foreword

As a longtime student of state land use policy and then Illinois resident, I watched with interest and envy when Maryland burst onto the national scene with its Smart Growth and Neighborhood Conservation initiative in 1997. Almost immediately, Maryland grabbed the spotlight from land use pioneers, such as Oregon, Florida, and New Jersey, and set forth a bold new approach based primarily on fiscal carrots and sticks. No one was certain whether it would work, but there was no denying Maryland had launched a bold new experiment and, fortunately, John Frece was there to record every detail.

Frece's account is a rare inside look at the process of land use policymaking at the state level. Although others have written about this subject before, never has the story been told by someone who attended all the key staff meetings, heard the private conversations between the governor and his adversaries, and himself played a key role in the dissemination and execution of the inspiring new approach. As a result, the stories are vivid, the dialogue is clear, and the insights are revealing.

The reader is hooked immediately as the story unfolds in Room 217 of the Annapolis State House. There the governor is peppering his staff: What new instruments should his new approach entail? How might they affect the various stakeholders? And, how should the details be released to the unrelenting press? As in a murder mystery, a cast of characters come alive: the determined and savvy Governor Glendening, the quiet but methodical Ron Krietner, the energetic and persuasive Ron Young, the cowboy John Griffin, the powerful and ambitious Cas Taylor, and the stubborn and conservative Ron Guns. Frece himself makes some cameo appearances as the governor's spokesman and one of the last to leave the post-Glendening Office of Smart Growth.

A surprising array of challenges faced by the Glendening administration is woven into the storyline. The owner of the newly arrived Baltimore Ravens demands a new stadium, creating an investment opportunity in urban revitalization. A big controversial development in Charles County enables the governor to grandstand for resource preservation. And Wal-Mart proposes a new store in historic Chestertown, to the chagrin of the governor, but just out of his state policy reach.

In the dramatic climax, and in a wonderful metaphor for the entire program, Glendening breaks a stalemate with Ron Guns by withholding the supplemental budget. In this crucial confrontation, of course, Glendening wins. But the electoral loss of Glendening's lieutenant governor, Kathleen Kennedy Townsend, to Robert Ehrlich brings to Annapolis the first Republican governor since Spiro Agnew, and Smart Growth suddenly faced a whole new set of interesting challenges.

But Frece's tale is much more than a great read on a long flight. It provides for serious students and policy analysts valuable lessons on the messy, fast moving, unpredictable, and always highly political environment in which state land use policy is made. Fortunately, Frece makes many of these lessons explicit in the final chapter. Among the most important: (1) *To be successful, elected leaders must wrap their substantive land use reforms within an aggressive communications and marketing strategy.* Governor Glendening, John Frece, and the state of Maryland changed the debate. The choice is not whether to grow or not to grow; the question is whether to grow smart. *(2) To make an incentive-based initiative work, you have to fund it.* The evidence thus far suggests Maryland has yet to win the war on sprawl. Whether the incentives were too small, inadequately maintained, or fundamentally inappropriate policy instrument remains to be seen. Finally, *(3) There is absolutely no substitute for having strong leadership from the top.* As the story makes clear, a governor can, with perseverance, timing, and dedicated staff, change the direction of land use policy for a state and perhaps for an entire nation. And in doing so, he can play the protagonist in a fascinating tale of sprawl and politics.

Gerrit-Jan Knaap
College Park, Maryland
February 2007

*Gerrit-Jan Knaap is Professor of Urban Studies and Planning and Executive Director of the National Center for Smart Growth Research and Education at the University of Maryland. Dr. Knaap's research interests include the economics and politics of land use planning, the efficacy of economic development instruments, and the impacts of environmental policy. He is co-author, editor, or co-editor of five books and numerous articles and papers on land use, land markets, and growth management in Oregon, Maryland, and elsewhere. He earned a BS from Willamette University, his MS and PhD from the University of Oregon, and received postdoctoral training at the University of Wisconsin-Madison, all in economics.*

# Chapter 1

# Room 217

Room 217 is a small windowless conference room on the second floor of the Maryland State House in Annapolis. A security guard sits outside the combination-controlled entrance from the hallway on one side. On the other, connected by a small vestibule just large enough for a loveseat, table and lamp, and a dormitory-sized refrigerator, is a private, "back door" entrance to the office of the governor of Maryland.

It is in Room 217 that the governor regularly meets with his staff and cabinet secretaries, legislators, or invited guests to discuss legislation, the formulation of state policy, or other issues. Though the photographs, plaques, and other memorabilia that adorn the walls of this somewhat airless room change from administration to administration, the function generally stays the same. The staff assembles at the appointed hour and waits for the governor to arrive and take his seat at the head of a long, narrow, dark wood table flanked with facing rows of upholstered chairs. From there he directs the discussion and asks the questions, which usually revolve around a detailed memo on the topic of the day sent to him in advance by members of his staff or state agencies.

It was in Room 217 in the spring and summer of 1996 that Maryland's Smart Growth initiative was born. But no one called it that at first.

It is improbable that any of the two dozen or more staff and cabinet secretaries who met in that room in different combinations throughout that year sensed they were doing anything especially momentous. Important to the governor's agenda? Yes. Necessary to bring some order to the chaotic development that had spread across Maryland over the last thirty to fifty years? Absolutely. But few could have imagined that the land use program that was later to be officially titled the "Smart Growth and Neighborhood Conservation" initiative would gain national and even international attention and catapult its principal proponent, Democratic governor Parris N. Glendening, into the national limelight.

**Fig. 1.1.** Democrat Parris N. Glendening served as Maryland's governor from 1995 until 2003. Photo courtesy of the *Baltimore Sun.*

Nor did those involved recognize at first the importance or lasting quality of the phrase "Smart Growth"—or that the very term "Smart Growth" would become so commonplace that it would evolve into a national shorthand for the broad set of concepts that include growth management, environmental protection, transportation and housing choice, walkable communities, fiscally responsible infrastructure investments, quality building design, farmland preservation, and more.

The program caught on fast, not only in Maryland, but around the country. Less than a year after the Smart Growth initiative was enacted, Keith Schneider, then executive director of the Michigan Land Use Institute, a growth management advocacy group based in the Traverse City region of Michigan, gushed in an article in the *Detroit Free Press* that "Maryland's Smart Growth program is the most promising new tool for managing growth in a generation."[1] Accolades from elsewhere around the country poured in, often before the new program had even developed a track record. This almost instant recognition was, in part, testament to the pent-up desire among environmentalists, urban planners, and others for state governments to step up their involvement in local land use decisions and growing concern about the detrimental effects of sprawl development. It had been twenty-five years or more since Oregon, Vermont, Hawaii, Colorado, and Florida first established their growth management efforts, and about fifteen since Washington, Florida, and Maryland had engaged in a second wave of land use measures.[2]

The praise coming Maryland's way also was sparked by the state's effort to shift the debate from "no growth" to "smart growth," that is, from opposing growth to trying to find a way to accommodate it; and, to Maryland's novel notion that growth could somehow be managed by state government using its financial support for development in certain specified areas, but not in others—an incentive-based approach rather than a more traditional regulatory approach.

The Smart Growth program that emerged from Room 217 at the end of 1996 was primarily the product of a governor who was both experienced with and interested in land use issues and who was determined to give state government a bigger say in local land use decisions. Leadership on this issue originated with the governor and never waned; in fact, the governor's personal determination to make Smart Growth a success built and strengthened with each new initiative, with each positive editorial, and with each passing year. Toward the end of his second term, Glendening used his position as chairman of the National Governors' Association to focus the attention of the nation's governors on growth issues and their relationship to the economy and quality of life. At some point before his first term was over, it dawned on Parris Glendening that Smart Growth would be his "legacy issue" as governor. A governor who came to office thinking he would make his mark with economic development or education realized the opportunity Smart Growth presented and he became determined to make the most of it. By the time he was elected governor in 1994, Glendening had been so routinely tied to development interests that he tried to change his image by listing more environmentalists on his campaign contributors' list.[3] But, when he left office eight years later, he had become so "green" that he felt comfortable giving his fellow governors copies of the Dr. Seuss children's book, *The Lorax.*

Maryland's Smart Growth program was also very much the work of a relatively new gubernatorial staff of planning, housing, transportation, economic development, and environmental officials who genuinely believed that past governmental policies had encouraged—even rewarded—costly and damaging sprawl development. A new policy approach, they reasoned, could reverse those trends. This approach was further shaped and strengthened by a team of top state agricultural and natural resource officials who had become increasingly alarmed at the rate that farmland and forests in Maryland were vanishing, the deterioration of the water quality and resources in the Chesapeake Bay and its tributaries, and loss of the scenic vistas that made the tidewater villages and the farms in the piedmont hills of rural Maryland so beautiful.

At the time, however, the emerging Smart Growth program was just another new policy initiative that the governor intended to advance along with others in the upcoming 1997 legislative session. Neither he nor anyone else suggested or even thought Smart Growth would become the centerpiece of his legislative package for 1997, much less the principal legacy of the two-term Glendening administration.

Cabinet secretaries—and even the governor himself—candidly, but privately, worried whether a statewide land use measure had any chance of passage in the General Assembly, where it faced certain opposition from county governments and other powerful interests. Some of the governor's political advisers went even farther, suggesting that even if Smart Growth did pass, no one would care. Compared with tax cuts, increased funding for education, or other potent pocketbook issues, Smart Growth seemed to them little more than a boutique issue of interest only to planners, government technocrats, and perhaps a handful of "greenies" from the environmental movement.

Moreover, it was risky, likely to generate division within the state's political establishment, especially at the local level, and opposition from home builders, developers, and the other moneyed interests in the private sector who largely financed political campaigns. It would probably take a lot of the governor's fast dwindling supply of political capital to get a Smart Growth proposal through the General Assembly and some of his cautious aides were asking one another whether it would be worth the effort.

For Glendening, a man who even before his first inauguration talked boldly (some would say presumptuously) about his plans to serve two full terms as governor and whose 1998 reelection campaign was already being charted and planned in early 1996, Smart Growth was, in retrospect, an unusual and unexpected policy for him to push.

## The Foundation for Land Use Management

It is tempting to look at Maryland's Smart Growth initiative out of context, as if it were a discrete program that suddenly burst on the scene in 1997. In fact, it was just the latest in a continuum of land use measures in Maryland that dated back more than sixty years. The foundation on which Maryland's Smart Growth program was built included, among other initiatives, the creation of the Maryland State Planning Commission in 1927, the oldest state planning commission in the country. By 1959, the commission staff became the State Planning Department and was subsequently elevated to cabinet status as the Department of State Planning. A steady stream of planning legislation followed: the State Planning Act of 1974, the Chesapeake Bay Critical Areas Act of 1984, and the Economic Growth, Resource Protection and Planning Act of 1992.

In a State of the State address to the Maryland General Assembly in 1973, Governor Marvin Mandel said: "One of the great issues facing Maryland today is the proper and wisest use of our rapidly diminishing land reserves. Orderly and balanced growth are no longer desirable goals. They are essential requirements if Maryland is to remain fit for human habitation." Those remarks predated the Smart Growth initiative by twenty-four years, yet sounded like words Parris Glendening might easily have uttered.

"I do not join with those who would pave over our State, those who would overdevelop and bury us under rows of drive-in restaurants and service stations at the sacrifice of openness and beauty, those whose fetish for asphalt and brick would deny us a blade of grass," said Mandel, a small, balding, old-school machine politician from Baltimore who might not have been expected to express such a personal connection with the natural beauty of rural Maryland.

After an obligatory statement professing that the state had no interest in usurping local government authority over land use decisions, Mandel nonetheless said, "I am convinced the State has a legitimate interest to protect. . . . I believe the State has every right to be concerned with—and a part of—decisions involving large developments that affect the State."

"Finally," he said, "I believe the State should take the lead in defining critical areas of Maryland—areas that should be preserved against encroachment, areas that would be damaged by improper development, over-development, and greater density of population. Yet we must plan with the thought in mind that we do not limit the availability of land so

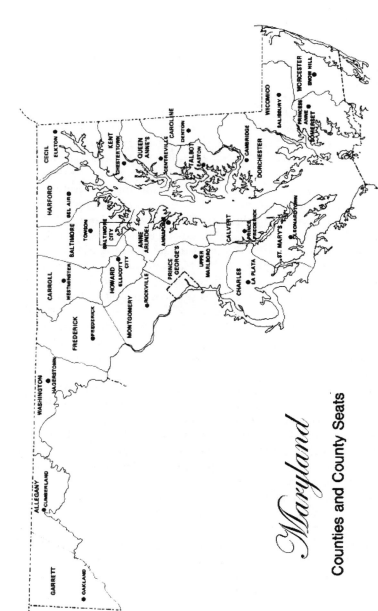

**Map 1.1.** The State of Maryland. Courtesy of the Maryland State Archives.

greatly that we inflate its price beyond the reach of those who would make good use of it."[4]

In the years since Mandel's term in office, Maryland has put in place an array of progressive environmental programs, including measures to protect both tidal and non-tidal wetlands, to preserve farmland, to purchase open space for parks, to regulate storm water runoff from development projects, and to require trees to be planted in place of those cut to make way for development.

Maryland citizens, relatively well educated, affluent, and, on most issues, politically progressive, generally supported these initiatives. That is probably because many of the proposals related to efforts to protect the Chesapeake Bay, which through the efforts of the Chesapeake Bay Foundation, Clean Water Action, and other groups has become an iconic symbol of the health of the environment and, by extension, the state's overall quality of life. How else to explain the state's acceptance of Governor Harry R. Hughes's Critical Areas law in 1984,[5] which for the first time placed constraints on development within a thousand feet of the entire shoreline of the Maryland portion of the bay and its tidal tributaries? The net effect of that single piece of legislation was, in essence, to downzone about 10 percent of the landmass of the state. Yet, Maryland citizens—with exceptions, of course—seemed to understand the purpose and support it. Increasingly, state leaders and the public began to acknowledge the connection between land use on the shore and water quality in the bay. Against this background, the Smart Growth effort seemed a logical next step.

## The 2020 Commission Debacle

Six years before Smart Growth, the General Assembly was asked to enact a proposal that would have shifted much of the authority over land use in Maryland from local governments to the state. Even though it failed, the Maryland Growth and Chesapeake Bay Protection Act of 1991[6] elevated the level of debate on land use issues, brought into question the fundamental assumption that most land use authority should reside at the local government level, and set in motion changes that would provide the foundation for the Smart Growth initiative.

The 2020 Commission work grew out of a regional compact to protect the Chesapeake Bay. Governor Hughes had convinced the governors of neighboring Pennsylvania and Virginia, the mayor of the District of Columbia, and the administrator of the U.S. Environmental Protection Agency, to meet on December 9, 1983, at George Mason University in Fairfax, Virginia, where they signed an agreement pledging to work together on bay issues.[7] It was the clearest recognition yet that the traditional parochial approach, with each state going its own way, would not adequately address the multiple influences that affected the health of the Chesapeake. The bay watershed stretches over more than 64,000 square miles in six states and the District of Columbia, includes 150 major rivers and streams, and extends from Southside Virginia as far north as Cooperstown, New York, and from the eastern mountains of West Virginia to the flat, sandy farm fields of Delaware.

In 1988, the members of this regional compact established a "2020 Panel" that was asked to produce a report on growth management regulations, environmental programs, and infrastructure requirements necessary to protect the bay through the year 2020, while still accommodating projected population growth in the region. The panel subsequently recommended six "visions" to guide policymakers as to how future development in the region should occur:

1.  Development is concentrated in suitable areas;
2.  Sensitive areas are protected;
3.  In rural areas, growth is directed to existing population centers and resource areas are protected;
4.  Stewardship of the Chesapeake Bay and the land is a universal ethic;
5.  Conservation of resources, including a reduction in resource consumption, is practiced; and,
6.  Funding mechanisms are addressed to achieve these visions.[8]

In early 1989, Governor William Donald Schaefer appointed Michael D. Barnes, a lawyer and former four-term congressman from Maryland's Washington suburbs, to head a "2020 Commission" that was to review the 2020 Panel's recommendations and determine their application to Maryland.

In November 1990, just after Governor Schaefer had been reelected to a second term and two months before the 1991 General Assembly was to convene, the Barnes Commission unveiled its recommendations. The sweeping proposal called for local governments to designate land in their jurisdictions in four categories: developed areas; growth areas; sensitive areas; and rural and resource areas. The commission also recommended that the state establish specified permitted densities and performance standards within the growth, developed, and rural resource areas, and require local governments to inventory their environmentally sensitive areas and develop protection programs. Finally, and perhaps most significantly, the commission proposed that the state be given approval authority over local plans, which then would remain valid for only three years.

It was a bold proposal to shift the balance of power over land use control in Maryland from the local level to a more shared responsibility with the state. Any seasoned legislative observer realized it would take months, if not years, for the General Assembly and affected local governments to absorb and react to the implications of such a drastic change. The ever-impatient Schaefer, nudged forward by the Barnes Commission members, never hesitated for a moment, throwing this piece of red meat to the lions in the legislature right after Christmas.

Schaefer met directly with Barnes and others on the 2020 Commission, who urged him to take immediate action, recalled Ronald M. Kreitner, the director of the Maryland Office of Planning and a member of the commission.[9] Jacqueline Rogers, then Schaefer's housing secretary, was among those pushing hardest for action, Kreitner later said. Others, however, counseled patience.

"It was an unwieldy way to develop it with that commission," recalled John R. Griffin, then the deputy secretary of Maryland's Department of Natural Resources.[10] Griffin said he drafted a memo for DNR Secretary Torrey C. Brown to send to Schaefer urging delay until the proposal's most controversial elements could be worked out. Compromises were possible, he thought, but they would take time. But Schaefer, a former mayor of Baltimore with a volcanic personality, the conviction that he knew best, and a slogan, "Do It Now," that summed up his approach to governance, would have none of it.

"We argued that we needed a year to go around and negotiate the details of that—don't just throw it into the legislature, but 'Mister Do It Now' threw it in there and got clobbered. We needed to do a lot of fine tuning and talk with people and negotiate it," Griffin said later.[11]

Even in progressive Maryland, the 2020 proposal went too far. "Response to the Barnes Commission bill was overwhelmingly negative," University of Maryland Professor James R. Cohen reports.[12] Though strongly supported by environmental groups, it was opposed by bankers, home builders, farmers, foresters, and, most vehemently of all, by county and municipal officials.[13] The 2020 Commission proposal seemed the clearest possible evidence that their long-held suspicion was true: the state was determined to take away local authority over land use decisions.

The Barnes Commission bill never emerged from committee, although it did not die without a fight. State Planning Director Kreitner, whose state agency served as commission staff, said that, in retrospect, the commission's openness may have been its undoing. The work of the commission had been so public and so widely disseminated, he said, that it gave opponents ample opportunity to develop strategies to fight it.

At the time, many opponents complained that the Barnes Commission recommendations failed because they had been worked out behind closed doors and sprung on the legislature at the last moment, but Kreitner called that argument "an absolutely bogus complaint."[14]

"One could actually say that the reverse was true," he later recalled. "What happened was that [opponents] got time to prepare. We had thirty-three members on the panel—we had people from MACO [the Maryland Association of Counties], MML [the Maryland Municipal League], the homebuilders, and others. All those people were there and they sat there and took the information out and rallied their troops against it."

Kreitner recalled how executives of the Rouse Company, the developers of the "new town" of Columbia, Md., showed up to oppose the bill at one committee hearing only to see the company's internationally known founder, James W. Rouse, seated in the audience waiting to testify in favor of the bill. The executives beat a hasty retreat, Kreitner recalled.

The longtime state planning director noted that the effort engendered strong editorial support from both the *Baltimore Sun* and the *Washington Post*, sharply raising the public dialogue on growth issues. It also produced products that would become prototypes for the Smart Growth battles later in the decade. For example, to make the case for stronger state land use authority, Kreitner's office spent hours preparing what he called the first "measles maps," which showed in splotchy red dots the dispersed development pattern that had become the statewide trend.

"The maps were critical. This was the first real use of a series of county level maps showing both changes in development and potential development based on approved subdivisions," Kreitner said. "MACO was vociferous in attacking them. One they attacked was the map of Caroline County. They tried to undermine our credibility by showing one point on the map they claimed wasn't really development, but was a farm manure holding facility." In the end, Kreitner said, the experience "underscored for me the need to have great data and great visual images."[15]

The Barnes Commission proposal sank, in part, because the timing was wrong. It arrived before the legislature the same session in which Schaefer introduced a mammoth and wildly controversial proposal to revamp the state's tax structure.[16] That, in turn, coincided with a downturn in the state and national economy. Schaefer was further distracted by a very public spat over tax policy with his lieutenant governor, Melvin A. Steinberg, and some of the governor's most loyal cabinet secretaries were split over whether to press forward with the Barnes recommendations or pull back and wait a year.

When the end finally came, it was a crushing defeat for advocates of stronger state authority over land use. It also served as a cautionary tale for subsequent political leaders who might otherwise be tempted to push for stronger state authority.

## The '92 Growth Act

Intent on rebounding from this rare loss, and politically looking for a way to save face, Governor Schaefer immediately pushed to pass a revised land use bill the following year, but one that was not nearly as forceful as the original 2020 Commission proposal. It was, by comparison, so diluted and inoffensive that even its something-for-everyone name ultimately had to be worked out by committee: the Economic Growth, Resource Protection and

Planning Act of 1992.[17] To try to assure the broadest possible legislative support, the bill explicitly affirmed the state's often conflicting "dual commitment to protect the environment and foster economic growth."*

The "Growth Act," as it came to be known, nevertheless managed to put in place some modest advances. It placed into statute the 2020 Panel's earlier six "Visions" to guide Maryland's future development, but attempted to mollify the opponents of the 1991 legislation by splicing in a new "Vision" between the old number 5 and number 6 designed to make clear the state's pro-growth position and to encourage the fast-tracking of development projects. The new number 6 read: "To assure the achievement of [Visions] 1 through 5 above, economic growth is encouraged and regulatory mechanisms are streamlined." Also added was an eighth "Vision" that stated, "Adequate public facilities and infrastructure under the control of the county or municipality are available or planned in areas where growth is to occur."

Perhaps the most important provision of the Growth Act was a requirement that all local government comprehensive plans be revised to be consistent with the Visions. The Growth Act also specifically identified four types of "sensitive areas" for special protection: streams and stream buffers; 100-year floodplains; habitats for endangered species; and steep slopes. But it was left to local governments to draft plans to protect these and other sensitive areas.

The Growth Act required local plans to contain recommendations that:

- Encourage streamlined review of development applications within areas designated for growth;
- Encourage the use of flexible development regulations to promote innovative and cost-saving site design and protect the environment;
- Use innovative techniques to foster economic development in areas designated for growth; and,
- Encourage more widespread use of flexible development standards.[18]

---

*Managing Maryland's Growth, What You Need to Know About Smart Growth and Neighborhood Conservation, Maryland Office of Planning, May 1997, 18. This approach was not unheard of. Other states had previously tried to tie together land use, environmental protection, and economic development goals, often within a single agency. Oregon, for example, created a Department of Land Conservation and Development. More recently, Massachusetts Governor Mitt Romney combined four major agencies, Environmental Affairs, Housing and Community Development, Transportation, and Energy Resources, into one super-agency, the Department of Commonwealth Development, with broad responsibility over issues related to growth management and the state's capital investment program.

Finally, the Growth Act created a seventeen-member advisory commission to monitor the progress made in implementing the new land use law, explore new solutions, and report annually to the governor and the General Assembly. Seats on the Growth Commission were designated to represent the full array of land use stakeholders: business, finance, agriculture, forestry, environmental, civic associations, planning, real estate development interests, counties and municipal governments, and the General Assembly.

For the next several years, the Growth Commission invested countless hours monitoring the land use actions of the state and its twenty-three counties. Relying on extensive staff support from the Maryland Office of Planning, the commission conducted studies, produced reports, and made recommendations to the governor and the General Assembly. It proposed revisions of "Article 66B," the state law that entrusts local governments with land use authority and proscribes the duties and limits of that authority.[19]

The '92 Growth Act, Kreitner believes, "started up a lot of processes for the state to examine [local] plans, set up a commission to monitor it, and generated a lot of stuff that was useful in '96 when we were trying to say we had to go the next step. It was pretty fundamental groundwork for getting something else in place in later years."[20]

Yet, in the final analysis, the Growth Commission was never more than a powerless advisory body. Despite solid research on Adequate Public Facilities Ordinances and other topics, without a champion in high political office, nothing the commission did or said could make the recipients of its reports listen or act. In later years, Governor Glendening and others considered revamping the commission to give it more authority and responsibility, but ultimately decided it was not worth the fight.

In 2002, after ten years, three chairmen, eight annual reports, and recommendations on public facility needs, modifications to the state planning law (Article 66B of the Annotated Code) and guidelines for transferable development rights, the governor and the General Assembly simply allowed the Growth Commission to "sunset" and go quietly out of existence.

## "Directed Growth"

Before there was "Smart Growth," there was "Directed Growth." At least that was the name Governor Glendening and his staff used internally as they set about the task of devising a policy that later would be known as "Smart Growth." The idea was simply to find ways to "direct growth" back to existing communities, which they thought would have the effect of "neighborhood conservation."[21]

For the governor and his staff to be able to focus on an issue such as land use took unusual discipline given the way everything else had gone for Glendening during his first fifteen difficult months as governor. His first year had been marred by a prolonged scandal involving lucrative pensions he and several of his top aides were to receive from Prince George's County, where he had served as county executive for twelve years before being elected governor in November 1994. Even his election had been controversial, with Glendening winning by a whisker-thin margin of only a few thousand absentee ballots and then surviving a court challenge by his Republican opponent that did not end until the eve of his inauguration.

By spring of 1996, Glendening had just completed an equally tumultuous second legislative session. He had been forced to use every resource and political strategy at his disposal to convince a reluctant General Assembly to ignore vehement citizen opposition and authorize the use of public funds for not one, but two professional sports stadiums. One was a new stadium to be built in downtown Baltimore for the city's new National Football League franchise, the recently arrived Cleveland Browns,* and the other was to provide highway and other improvements for the Washington Redskins' new stadium in suburban Prince George's County outside of Washington, D.C. The two projects were enormously contentious and complicated by the problem that every argument the governor and his staff made for one of the projects (e.g., publicly built, in the city) was contradicted by the facts of the other (e.g., privately built, in the suburbs). Members of the governor's own political party were among his loudest critics, claiming he was using taxpayer dollars to enrich already rich sports team owners. The clash was ugly. Governor Glendening had further polarized members of the General Assembly—and the public—that year by making good on a major campaign promise to push through tougher gun control legislation. While many cheered the effort, his popularity rating, both inside the legislature and out, began dropping fast.

There was no end to the other controversial or difficult issues on the new governor's plate. Yet, as far as the public or even legislators knew, none of them had anything to do with land use. Instead, they saw an administration embroiled in a freight controversy with Conrail, and fighting environmental groups who opposed administration plans to dump spoil dredged from the port of Baltimore's shipping channel into the deepest recesses of the Chesapeake Bay. The governor found himself trying to prevent political defections from conservative, rural Democrats, fending off criticism of his aggressive fundraising tactics, engaging in school funding squabbles with Baltimore's mayor, and trying to find solutions to problems as different as having too few blue crabs in the Bay and too many black bears in the state's western mountains. There was a sense the administration was spinning out of control and the internal pressure to reverse the trend was daunting.

---

*Subsequently renamed the Baltimore Ravens.

Insiders, however, knew that land use issues were definitely on the governor's mind. In his first months in office in 1995, Glendening had begun to probe for ways the state could more aggressively involve itself in local land use decisions. But, as someone who had spent most of his political career in local government—three terms as county executive of a major metropolitan jurisdiction, eight years before that on the county council, and two years before that as a city councilman in the old streetcar suburb of Hyattsville—Governor Glendening knew from experience and instinct that tampering with the balance of power over land use could be politically explosive. So, he worked on the issue steadily, but quietly.

In his inaugural year, the governor held a series of internal meetings with his cabinet and staff to focus them collectively on the issue of revitalization. The governor's experiences in Hyattsville, though nearly two decades old by then, were still fresh in his mind. There, he was later to say, he watched helplessly as the county and the state consistently funded transportation, sewer and water, school construction, and other infrastructure or services to support new development, but rarely if ever turned their attention or resources toward older, inner-Beltway communities such as Hyattsville. The opportunity for revitalization was being lost, he thought. He felt he was getting little or no help to stem the steady deterioration of his community.

The areas he had represented, the areas he still identified with, were areas often populated by blacks, Hispanics, or other recent immigrants or whites of modest income. They were not sharing equally in the wealth of the state, the governor believed. These areas, he said, were often poor, working-class neighborhoods long neglected by state and county governments and in need of a helping hand.

Nor was it lost on the politically attuned governor that these areas—spread among the used car lots and tired strip malls that lined bedraggled U.S. Route 1 just south of the University of Maryland campus at College Park and hard against the state's border with Washington, D.C.—also generally tended to vote Democratic. They were the areas that had given him his narrow margin of victory. These older parts of the state needed help. They had helped make him governor, and now he was looking for ways to return the favor. He decided to focus the attention of his entire cabinet on the issue of revitalization.

A decade later, some of Glendening's detractors held that all he had cared about was rural land preservation. That was not true. There is no question the Glendening administration was extraordinarily successful in protecting farms and other rural lands from encroaching development. Yet the idea of revitalizing the state's older communities was the new governor's first goal and a concept that was the starting point for and remained the backbone of his Smart Growth initiative for the remainder of his term.

In retrospect, it is significant that the governor did not single out one department, say the Department of Housing and Community Development or perhaps the Department of Business and Economic Development, to address the issue of revitalization. Instead, from the outset, he encouraged a cross-departmental, team approach. What could the administration as a whole do to encourage revitalization? How could the administration as a whole direct new growth to older established communities? As the Smart Growth program was to build and expand in later years, this concept of cross-departmental cooperation and collaboration would become a hallmark of the initiative.*

In mid-December 1995, the governor's cabinet convened one last time before the start of the 1996 legislative session, meeting at the Johns Hopkins Hospital on North Caroline Street in East Baltimore. Housing Secretary Patricia Payne welcomed the cabinet to Baltimore for what was billed as a "Cabinet Revitalization and Directed Growth Strategy Meeting."[22] Lt. Gov. Kathleen Kennedy Townsend spoke, as did Glendening's secretary of state and chief political adviser, John T. Willis.

The all-day event featured briefings by Kreitner, the Maryland Historic Trust's Bill Pencek, and Maryland Department of Transportation planner Henry Kay. Part of the morning was spent touring East Baltimore neighborhoods with Baltimore Delegate Hattie N. Harrison and Scot T. Spencer, then with the Historic East Baltimore Community Action Coalition. In the afternoon, a team of facilitators from Andersen Consulting led the cabinet through four hours of discussions designed to identify a statewide, interagency "revitalization and directed growth strategy."

At that session, David L. Winstead, a land use attorney who had been brought into the new administration to serve as Glendening's secretary of transportation, suggested there may be "a role for state 'carrots' as incentives to directed growth."[23] It was an image that would stick. Once the legislative session was over, that concept—the idea of using government incentives as a means of influencing where new growth occurs—would become the primary land use strategy the governor and his cabinet and staff would focus on for the remainder of 1996.

In later years, Governor Glendening would use photographs of bright orange carrots to help explain how he intended the Maryland Smart Growth program to work.

---

*Cross-departmental collaboration, for example, was identified as one of the achievements of the Smart Growth initiative in a study of the program performed by the European-based Organization for Economic Co-operation and Development (OECD), The Maryland *Smart Growth Initiative: A Thematic Policy Review*, 9th Session of the Territorial Development Policy Committee, Martigny, Switzerland, June 27, 2003.

# Chapter 2

# Brownfields, Chapman's Landing, and the Chestertown Wal-Mart

Parris Glendening's 1994 campaign for governor revolved around what he called "the 5 E's"—Education, Economic Development, Excellence in Government, Enforcement, and Environment. But while his campaign rhetoric hit on all five "E's," he seemed most passionate about becoming a governor known for creating jobs and boosting the state's economy.

"When Parris came into office, he ran on this strong platform of economic development," recalled John R. Griffin, who became Glendening's secretary of Natural Resources in late winter of 1995. "There really wasn't much in those five "E's" under "Environment" in terms of land use. Remember, Parris had been criticized during his campaign for being way too close to developers."[1]

Griffin, whose own political upbringing began in Prince George's County, recalled Glendening's reputation there: "He really wasn't an environmentalist in the county," he recalled. "He did what he had to do, but it wasn't something that had captured his soul, certainly."

To demonstrate his focus on the economy, Glendening recruited James T. Brady, a gruff but determined businessman from Baltimore, to head the state's Department of Business and Economic Development. Brady had been managing partner of the Baltimore office of Arthur Andersen LLP. He was wealthy, successful, and well connected in the business community. (Some on Glendening's staff referred to Brady behind his back as "Diamond Jim.")

"Glendening really courted him because Parris was really high on economic development, jobs and all of that. He wanted someone who would personify all that in the eyes of the business community, and he found Brady," recalled Griffin. "And I remember in the first year or so, at cabinet meetings, [Glendening] basically said, 'Brady's my man.' And

**Fig. 2.1.** Hard charging Baltimore business executive James T. Brady was tapped by Glendening to be his first economic development secretary. Photo courtesy of the *Baltimore Sun*.

Brady's expectations from having been recruited were essentially that he would be at the right hand of the throne. Brady would be a super-cabinet member and everything would be analyzed in terms of how it would help the economy of Maryland. And he would be his top cabinet adviser. He'd be there for everything, calling the shots for Parris, the whole bit, sort of like a chief of staff almost."

But it did not take long for Glendening, Griffin believes, to begin to realize "there wasn't the political payoff for him to be the economic development governor, principally because most of the businessmen didn't like him—that is, those who were not developers. And, they tended to be Republican. So, he didn't find the personal reinforcement with them that he started to find as he became an environmentalist."* – Politics

Still, at the beginning of 1996, Glendening was still touting issues he thought would resonate with the business community and one of them was the then somewhat obscure issue of brownfield redevelopment. The governor said he wanted to announce in his upcoming State of the State address his intention to introduce legislation that would make it easier to redevelop brownfield sites. But, in doing so, the governor used a somewhat environmental justification: "It can reduce sprawl and help revitalize our older areas," he explained to his staff.[2]

The concept of brownfield cleanup and redevelopment was still relatively new in Maryland in 1996, although states such as Michigan and New Jersey had been dealing effectively with brownfield issues for several years by then. The phrase referred to old industrial or manufacturing sites that were contaminated or thought to be contaminated by toxic chemicals. These sites, most of which in Maryland were located in older urbanized areas such as Baltimore or Cumberland, were hard to sell and rarely, if ever, cleaned up and redeveloped. They were unwanted remnants of the manufacturing economy that had flourished in Baltimore and other major American cities during most of the twentieth century, but which had largely been supplanted by a service and information technology economy by the time Glendening became governor. Land developers were afraid of being stuck with legal liability for the cost of cleaning up the contamination on brownfield sites or for any health effects that might result from the contamination. So, most of these sites, often located in the heart of otherwise urbanized areas, sat idle and abandoned, while new development moved out to the suburbs instead.

---

*Glendening's sour relationship with the business community sank to its lowest point later in his first term when the business community sued him over Executive Order 01.01.1996.13, which he issued in 1996, authorizing collective bargaining for state employees within the executive department.

By 1996, the issue had grown to such prominence that the Maryland business and development community made passage of brownfield legislation a priority. It, therefore, also became a priority of Secretary Brady. What business executives specifically wanted was protection against legal liability for the contamination caused by previous property owners. Why should they be penalized for purchasing or trying to clean up property contaminated by others?

But Maryland's powerful environmental groups reacted with suspicion. They were concerned that the liability protection sought by the business community would somehow provide legal protection for polluters. Worse, they were concerned that no one would be held responsible for the cost of cleaning up the contamination: not the original polluters, who either could not be found or identified or who had gone bankrupt and therefore had no assets with which to cover the cost of a cleanup; nor the subsequent buyers, who would be protected by the proposed legislation. Why should taxpayers subsidize the cleanup of these sites? Liability protection, they feared, meant no one but innocent taxpayers would be on the hook for either the cost of the cleanup or any subsequent spread of contamination or health problems that might occur. The potential magnitude of such costs could be staggering. If the state failed to appropriate enough money, the result might be little or no cleanup at all. Finally, the environmentalists were concerned that in their desire to help businesses return brownfield sites to productive use, the state would fail to insist upon thorough cleanup of contaminated sites.

To respond to these concerns, Governor Glendening assigned his new secretary of the environment, a former Chesapeake Bay Foundation executive named Jane Nishida, to try to find a middle ground. But just as the war between the environmentalists and the business community over brownfields legislation began to heat up, the issue became further complicated by gubernatorial politics.

Although Governor Glendening was only beginning his second year in office, some politicians in Maryland—including members of the governor's own party—already thought he was politically vulnerable. One highly ranked Democrat who had his eye on the governor's office was the Speaker of the House of Delegates, Casper R. Taylor Jr. of Allegany County. A somewhat portly, balding tavern owner from the mountains of Western Maryland—described in one newspaper profile as resembling "a doleful penguin"—Taylor had gradually worked his way up the legislative ladder to a committee chairmanship and finally to the top position in the House. Although politically savvy, he seemed overly ambitious for someone with such a small, rural, and distant political base. Nevertheless, as the 1996 session began, it became increasingly clear that Speaker Taylor was not going to go out of his way to help Governor Glendening look successful.

**Fig. 2.2.** Like many others during Glendening's difficult first term, House Speaker Casper R. Taylor, Jr., thought the new governor might be politically vulnerable. Photo courtesy of the *Baltimore Sun*.

In early January, Secretary Nishida called a meeting at her Baltimore offices to try to bring the environmentalists and the business community together on the brownfields issue. But before the meeting could even take place, Speaker Taylor and his Environmental Matters Committee chairman, conservative Cecil County Delegate Ronald A. Guns, called their own brownfields meeting in Annapolis. Privately, Governor Glendening steamed, complaining the legislators had "pre-empted Jane's meeting" and that the Speaker was "trying to capture the issue. They're not working cooperatively. They've started [their own] workgroup."[3]

## Chapman's Landing

Brownfields was not the only land use issue bothering the governor that winter. In Charles County, a historically rural tobacco farming county southeast of Washington that was fast becoming a suburban bedroom community for the nation's capital, developers were about to break ground on one of the largest new developments the county had ever seen. Chapman's Landing was to be a 4,600 unit planned development carved out of a 2,225 acre wooded tract along the Potomac River near Indian Head, north of Mattawoman Creek and roughly across the river from George Washington's Mount Vernon estate. The project would create a mini-city of about twelve thousand new residents twenty miles from Washington in a county that, at the time, had a population of about 115,000. It would include about 2.25 million square feet of commercial space and a two hundred acre golf course.

To some, this was the best and most extensively planned development ever proposed in Charles County. Different aspects of the project had been approved by two successive county boards of commissioners. The project was located within the growth area designated as part of the Charles County comprehensive plan. And the project's legal and development team were politically well connected. In his first year in office, Governor Glendening and his powerful chief of staff, Major F. Riddick Jr., worked hard to expedite required state approvals to get the Chapman's Landing project off the ground.

"They needed wetlands licenses, which at the time were still within DNR," Griffin recalled.* The developers of Chapman's were represented by George Brugger, a prominent Prince George's County land use lawyer who had donated money to Glendening's election campaigns and was

---

*Under Governor William Donald Schaefer, most of the authority over the issuance of environmental permits was transferred from DNR to the Maryland Department of Environment. On Griffin's recommendations, authority to issue permits required by developers before they could legally fill and/or build on wetlands was subsequently transferred from DNR to MDE during Glendening's first term.

close to Andrea Leahy-Fucheck, who had become the chief legal counsel to the new governor of Maryland. "Brugger came to see Major Riddick early in the first year about needing help from us with these permits. So, Major called me over [to Riddick's second floor State House office] to meet with Brugger and said, 'I want you to work with Brugger and the developer and I want monthly status reports, in writing.' I said, 'Okay.'"[4]

About the same time, however, statewide environmental groups and Southern Maryland environmentalists led by a determined activist named Bonnie Bick began to bombard the State House press corps with accusations about the environmental damage that would be wrought if Chapman's Landing were to be built. With increasing intensity, they complained that Chapman's was too big, would have too many adverse impacts on traffic and air and water quality, and would be built in an old-growth forest that ought to be protected, not developed. They worried aloud about the songbirds that would soon lose their habitat. Historic preservationists joined in the fight, saying they wanted to protect a nineteenth-century manor house on the property known as Mount Aventine. They cited growing concerns among existing Charles County residents that the drinking water table was falling, that wells at some homes were already drying up, and that the water withdrawal required by the Chapman's project could prove disastrous.

To the state's environmental community, Chapman's Landing ceased to be merely a development project they opposed; rather, it quickly grew into much more: a symbol of overdevelopment everywhere, and of large-scale development planned for the wrong place. It, quite literally, became their poster child representing the evils of development set against the virtues of natural resource protection. Steadily, swiftly, relentlessly, their campaign spread. Full-color posters picturing the dense green underbrush of the Chapman forest were distributed. "Save Chapman's Forest" first became a slogan; then it became a crusade.

The *Baltimore Sun* sent its environmental reporter to interview Griffin. "The land use issues were really starting to come out of this," Griffin recalled. "I said [to the reporter], 'I think it is time that we start taking a look at how counties do their land use when it comes to environmental impacts because this may be a classic example. The county thought it was doing the right thing. They went through a two- or three-year master planning process, debated the issues and a decided this would be their growth area.'"[5]

"I was trying to defend what we were trying to do. I said this was a priority project for the State House. I was honest with him about the status reports, and all of this showed up in the newspaper. And Parris calls me on the phone, very unhappy with me, and asks, 'Why was I doing status reports to Major Riddick?' We had a fairly heated discussion. I said, 'Because he asked me for them. He's your chief of staff, Governor. What the hell do you want me to do?'"

Griffin said after they had talked for awhile, he said, "Look, governor, stay on the phone with me for a minute and listen to me. You need to start to work on some better policies to guide local land use and zoning and this illustrates some of the problems inherent in the system as it exists." This, Griffin later recalled, "was the first time I ever talked to him about, quote, 'Smart Growth.'"[6]

Griffin said he and Mike Slattery, who then headed the non-tidal wetlands permit program for DNR, had reviewed the Chapman's Landing wetlands application and found it to be surprisingly good.

"As it turned out, we were all very satisfied with the concessions and the commitments that we had gotten out of the developer," Griffin recalled. "And we were getting ready to give them the wetlands licenses. They had done an extraordinarily good job." But by this point, with the environmentalists and the press both turning up the heat, the governor of Maryland was having second thoughts about his early support for Chapman's and was quietly suggesting that one way to stop the project would be for DNR to deny the wetlands permits.

"I said denying the environmental permits to stop a land use decision is wrong," Griffin recalled of his conversation with the governor. "I said the basic questions about where to grow and where to develop should be answered on the broader scale. I've got the permits, but that's just to handle some of the details about how it is done, not whether it should be done. So, I had a long discussion with him on the phone and a subsequent discussion with him in person when I advocated pretty strongly that he start to look at how you change state law to become more involved in local zoning and land use."[7]

"I did feel like I had some impact on him," Griffin said years later. "He was really worried about it. He was really upset by this article [in the *Sun*]."

"I'm frustrated," the governor told staff as he prepared for a private meeting with environmentalists in late February to discuss Chapman's. "It shouldn't be a growth area. The law is weak. The state should provide planning support (because) it is in the designated growth area, it passed the county plan, it passed county zoning. I cannot act arbitrarily when everyone follows the law. But it is illustrative of the frustration I, as the top official, have when the decision is made following the law. Now, I can't arbitrarily overturn it."[8]

The environmentalists, representing the Sierra Club, the Chesapeake Bay Foundation, and Clean Water Action, urged the governor to launch a comprehensive environmental impact study, to look at wetlands loss, water withdrawal, traffic generation, loss of forest cover, destruction of historic sites, even the health of the recently restored bass fishery in nearby Mattawoman Bay.

"I am really frustrated by the whole thing," the governor told them. "I will go back in my personal time and study this. Part of my difficulty, unfortunately, is that the pieces are in place based on a rather weak law. They followed the process. And Charles County officials are for it."[9]

The other issue that arose was whether Charles County had sufficient sources of drinking water to support such a large development. A number of wells in Charles County had gone dry and environmentalists were not the only ones who claimed the Chapman's development would only exacerbate the problem. In June 1997, Virginia U.S. Senator Charles S. Robb, Congressman James P. Moran, and State Senator Joseph V. Gartlan Jr., all wrote letters to the U.S. Army Corps of Engineers expressing concern about the impact that Chapman's might have on the availability of drinking water on the Virginia side of the Potomac.[10] A study by consultants hired by Charles County said there should be enough water for the county through 2020, but could not accurately predict beyond that.[11]

Later that summer, in a confidential memo to Nishida and senior counselor Eleanor Carey, a Baltimore lawyer the governor had recruited to his staff in October 1996, the governor's communications director, John W. Frece, said, "The issue surrounding Chapman's Landing has changed since the Governor last considered the project due to his embrace of the Smart Growth legislation."[12] The Smart Growth legislation had not even gone into effect, but Frece said, "The question is already being asked: 'How can [Glendening] say he is in favor of Smart Growth and at the same time support this project?'"[13]

The fight over Chapman's Landing played out agonizingly for another two years, until almost the eve of the 1998 election in which Glendening would seek reelection to a second term. By then, the governor had completely reversed field, deciding the environmentalists were right: Chapman's would be a blight on the landscape. He concluded the only solution was for the state to buy it, almost regardless of cost.

Brady, who had become so fed up with Glendening that he resigned from the cabinet in the spring of 1998, was quoted in stories about the Chapman's sale as saying the governor's change of heart had little to do with Smart Growth and much to do with winning over environmentalists in an election year.[14]

"As Parris gradually started moving away from economic development as the centerpiece of his administration, Brady got more and more disaffected," said Griffin, who often discussed the governor's shifting priorities with his fellow cabinet secretary. "He felt Parris basically set him up and pulled the rug out from under him."

"But I think Parris was looking for something—desperately looking for a cause."[15]

## The Wal-Mart in Chestertown

Across the bay on Maryland's Upper Eastern Shore, in the quaint eighteenth-century community of Chestertown, another land use issue over which the state seemingly had little authority had cropped up. Wal-Mart, the giant Arkansas-based merchandiser, had announced plans to build a 107,000 square foot store on the outskirts of town.

Now three hundred years old, Chestertown lines the banks of the upper reaches of the Chester River and was a prominent early inland trading port on Maryland's Eastern Shore. Washington College, the tenth-oldest liberal arts college in America, was founded there in 1782. The Kent County courthouse downtown dates to the 1860s and the Georgian, Federalist, and Victorian architecture along the town's streets takes visitors back in time.[16]

Chestertown's mayor and town leaders immediately recognized the threat Wal-Mart presented, fearing the effect such price competition would have on the town's small-scale, homegrown merchants. They could envision their graceful town's stately brick and white clapboard homes interspersed with abandoned and boarded up stores and its brick sidewalks empty. Moreover, the proposed Wal-Mart site, reachable only by car, was not even connected to the town's water and sewer lines. Wal-Mart was not the kind of company to take "no" for an answer, so some local political leaders looked to Annapolis for help.

But just as with Chapman's Landing, there seemed to be little the state could do about the Wal-Mart in Chestertown. It was, simply stated, a local issue. Even if the state could intervene, the governor and his staff faced the legitimate policy question of whether they *should* intervene. Municipal officials might want the state to become involved in this case, but what about the next case? What about the precedent that would be established by state intervention?

As the 1996 legislative session was drawing to a close, issues such as brownfields, Chapman's Landing, and the Chestertown Wal-Mart were beginning to blend in the same political stew and the concoction was beginning to simmer. On March 19, the governor met with Kreitner, his planning director, and Gene Lynch, his general services secretary, to talk about what to do. Kreitner emphasized the need for revitalization, saying growth could not be redirected from places like Chapman's without giving it some place to go, and that meant the state had to step up its efforts to revitalize older communities. Lynch talked about ways the state could capitalize on the value of state offices or facilities by intentionally placing them in revitalization areas as catalysts to new development—even in deteriorated areas shunned by other developers because of crime or other problems.[17]

"The biggest challenge will be public education. The public needs to think more about tradeoffs," Glendening replied. He added that as soon as the legislative session adjourned, he wanted to issue an executive order to set up a new growth commission or "something that strengthens considerably [the state's role in] growth management."

"Look at Chapman's Landing," the governor said two years before the state was to purchase the property. "There is nothing we should do to stop it. They followed every rule. But the dilemma is it is a nonsensical project. We need to change the rules. In '97, I want a whole series of tools—a package."[18]

# Chapter 3

# "Tell Them, 'The Governor Is Very Serious'"

Six days before *sine die*, the final day of the 1996 legislative session, Governor Glendening was already plotting his plans for the 1997 legislative session.
"I want subcabinet input on managing and controlling growth," he said on April 2. He added that he wanted a list of what the state had already done, what the state was currently doing, and what could be done to give the state more authority. "We know it needs teeth," he said.[1]

The first piece of what was to become the Smart Growth initiative arrived sooner than expected. On April 8, the final day of the legislative session, a last-ditch attempt to reach accord between environmentalists and the business community on the brownfields legislation fell apart. At 11 p.m., with only an hour remaining in the ninety-day session, the governor summoned to Room 217 the House and Senate conferees on the bill—Senators Brian Frosh, Michael Collins, and Clarence Blount and Delegates John Hurson, Anita Stup, and Ronald Guns—to see if a compromise could be found in time to revive the brownfields bill.

The Senate version of the bill, guided principally by Frosh, was generally backed by the environmentalists and focused on regulating brownfield cleanup; the House version, pushed by Guns, was backed by the business community and focused on providing financial incentives to developers to encourage brownfield redevelopment.

The six legislators said they saw no chance for compromise. Frosh, a senator from Bethesda, a densely developed and wealthy suburb of Washington, D.C., just over the Maryland line in Montgomery County, was the leading environmental voice in the General Assembly. He said passage of the House version of the bill was impossible, describing it as "too narrow." "It won't work," he said. Stup agreed, saying there was no way it would pass and no time left for further negotiation.[2]

**Fig. 3.1.** House Environmental Matters Committee Chairman Ronald Guns (left) and Senator Brian Frosh frequently clashed over environmental protection and Smart Growth issues. Photo courtesy of the *Baltimore Sun*.

This version was being pushed by Guns, the conservative who had chaired the House Environmental Matters Committee since 1991. A Vietnam vet who worked for the telephone company, Guns was elected to the House in 1983 representing five rural counties on the Upper Eastern Shore. He was generally viewed by the environmental community as the principal obstacle to passage of environmental protection legislation.*

Senator Blount, an elderly, stately, veteran lawmaker from Baltimore, intoned in his deep, soothing voice: "In twenty-five years, this is not the most difficult bill. It represents two hymnals created as part of the same church." Turning to Glendening, he said, "The only way for it to happen is for you to come up with one bill. You provide that leadership, we'll work with you."³

With those words that night, the first component of the growth management initiative the governor was already planning on introducing the following year was put in place. The governor would champion brownfields legislation in 1997, with plans to turn this legislative defeat into a gubernatorial political victory.

## The "Directed Growth" Workgroup

Once the session was over, the pace and depth of discussion of growth issues accelerated. The day after the lawmakers adjourned *sine die*, the "Directed Growth" staff convened to discuss the tools already in place and new ideas that might be added. Before the year was out, the governor, and/or members of his cabinet and staff would meet more than thirty times—often for hours at a time and in one instance for a full day—to shape and reshape the new initiative.

As they convened in Room 217 or exchanged ideas by e-mail, it became clear almost immediately that no one dared propose a 2020-style state assumption of land use authority. That lesson had been learned in 1991.

"This approach differs from 2020," said Deputy Natural Resources Secretary Ronald N. Young on April 9, 1996. "Actions taken now are incentives. The message is: The state is getting its own house in order. We're not taking over [authority from] the counties."⁴

Young would play a critical role throughout 1996 convincing outside groups to get on board the governor's emerging land use initiative. More importantly, Young was bursting with ideas and many of them became attached to various segments of the program as it took shape. Young had been a four-term mayor of Frederick, Maryland, from 1974 to 1990 and a

---

*By 2001, Glendening became so frustrated with his inability to push environmental legislation past Guns and his committee that he removed this roadblock within the General Assembly by appointing Guns to the utility-regulating Public Service Commission.

one-time candidate for lieutenant governor before being brought into state government by Governor Schaefer, another former mayor. To the regular irritation of many of his colleagues, Young still possessed the "do-it-my-way" attitude that is typical of many mayors. Despite his occasional abrasiveness, Young would go on to become one of the most influential and persuasive voices within the small Smart Growth planning group. It was a role he performed until he finally left state service in 2002.

As early as April 15, 1996, Glendening's staff drafted an executive order for him to sign that would have created a Cabinet Council on Directed Growth, Revitalization, and Neighborhood Conservation.

"In light of shrinking budgetary resources and increased demands for services, the need is greater than ever to ensure that private and public resources are directed in a manner to ensure existing infrastructures and assets are utilized to their fullest extent, that sprawl is minimized, that opportunities for economic development are maximized, that our natural resources are protected, and that we maintain, rejuvenate, and revitalize our neighborhoods, particularly in those areas most suitable for growth," the draft executive order stated.[5]

It would have created an eleven-member cabinet-level council that was to identify and make recommendations to the governor regarding "changes in state laws, regulations, investments, policies and programs to promote the State's directed growth, revitalization and neighborhood conservation initiative." Although this executive order was never signed, the proposed council was essentially a precursor for the Smart Growth Sub-Cabinet that Glendening would create by executive order two years later and use with increasing effectiveness for the remainder of his second term.

Glendening met with his sub-cabinet workgroup on "Directed Growth" on April 18 and began laying out the political strategy:

First, he said, "We need to build a broad coalition and consensus for this." Next, he said, "We can make the municipalities our natural allies in this." Third, he knew the proposal could not be seen as only an environmental program. "We need it to be strong pro-business," he said. And, he knew it would go nowhere without public support. "We need [to stress] the public impact. We need to raise visibility."[6]

Strategically, the governor was worried that others would come forward with their own land use proposals that would compete for attention with his and ultimately result in a diluted, lowest common denominator compromise.

"Ask everyone to hold back on other proposals," he told his staff. "Tell CBF [the Chesapeake Bay Foundation], 'The governor is going to make them happy. He's going to put the resources of his office on the line. Things will go through. Only they will cause it to collapse if there is division in our ranks. They have to know the game plan—that we're all heading in the same direction. [Tell them] there will be a major focus. We'll build a coalition and consensus. We'll have a [legislative] package by September."[7]

The governor also emphasized the importance of pulling together a rural-urban coalition to back the effort. "People who are fanatically interested in protecting the natural areas should be equally interested in protecting the urban areas," he said in a line he was later to use frequently in speeches.[8]

Members of the workgroup then began tossing out ideas, some of which would show up in the final Smart Growth program. Kreitner, the state planning director, suggested that new growth be constrained within boundaries drawn by local governments. Young suggested targeting state tax incentives to those defined growth areas. Jim Fielder, a deputy secretary for business and economic development who sat in for Brady, emphasized the need for brownfields legislation and also said local governments would be more supportive of targeted state assistance if they better understood the cost of providing infrastructure for growth.

The governor ended the meeting by directing everyone in the workgroup to develop lists of their "three top ideas" and "three secondary ideas." Among other details, he said they needed to "think through" what the initiative should be named.[9]

Pat Payne, the housing secretary, was dispatched to try to obtain a grant from the nonprofit Abell Foundation in Baltimore to finance a public education campaign to help sell the initiative to the public and, by doing so, to the legislature. Nishida, the environment secretary, was directed to counsel the Chesapeake Bay Foundation to be cooperative. "Tell them this is a one-stop opportunity. They can't blow it," the governor instructed.[10]

Glendening said he envisioned a program on which both Senator Frosh, the liberal voice of the environmentalists, and Delegate Guns, the conservative voice of the business community, could agree. "Get them to unite behind one bill. That is conceptually what we want to do," he said.[11]

The original list of "bold ideas" included suggestions for Oregon-style Urban Growth Boundaries, prioritizing public school funding in revitalization areas, protecting farming from nuisance suits with "right to farm" legislation, developing a system of transferable development rights (TDRs), establishing a "Directed Growth Superfund" to pay for infrastructure improvements, targeting tax incentives to locally designated growth areas, passing brownfields legislation, and renaming and redirecting the Growth Commission.

By early May, details began to fall in place. Growth areas would be constrained by the availability of water and sewer service. Farms would be excluded. Certain areas would be grandfathered. Local governments would still retain the authority to decide where development would go, but the state would decide when state financial assistance would be available.

"We're letting the jurisdictions make the choice, but we're not [necessarily] going to contribute to it," explained Nishida.[12]

A more structured outreach plan was developed, listing the individuals the governor would speak to personally and how the staff would deal with the two organizations that represented local government: the Maryland Municipal League and the Maryland Association of Counties. Specific assignments were handed out for staff to talk with the Maryland Farm Bureau, the Maryland Home Builders Association, the Chesapeake Bay Foundation, Clean Water Action, the mayor of Baltimore, legislative committee chairmen, and other powerful senators and delegates.

Central to the strategy was a plan to solicit advice rather than suggest solutions. This would calm some nerves and it might build some buy-in from those who gave ideas. It would also give the staff a clearer idea what the limits were—how far the state might dare to go.

"You can say, 'The governor is very serious about wanting to do something. Very serious. Tell us how to do it,'" he suggested.[13]

## CBF:  Arm's Length Support

At the same time, the governor wanted to develop a drumbeat of support on the editorial pages of the state's newspapers—an outcome he always mistakenly thought was easy to accomplish. He said he wanted the editorials to say, "The governor's right—there's a huge problem."[14] From that, he hoped to generate support for a solution.

One of the most likely centers of support was the environmental community in general and the Chesapeake Bay Foundation in particular.

Will Baker, CBF's wily president, understood better than most how delicate were the politics of land use in Maryland. Baker had been a leader in the effort to get the Barnes Commission recommendations approved five years earlier and he was still smarting from that defeat. He rued the day CBF had backed the '92 Growth Act, the flimsy substitute that one environmentalist at the time bitterly dismissed as "a nothing-burger."

Privately, Baker came to the State House to meet with Frece, then Glendening's communications director and one of several people on the governor's staff trying to shape the public message that would accompany the "Directed Growth" initiative. The Bay Foundation, Baker said with dead seriousness, had done a lot of work on this issue and was pretty defensive about others moving onto that turf. At the same time, however, CBF wanted something meaningful to pass and knew it could not do it on its own. More than that, Baker said, CBF recognized that if the initiative were seen as coming from CBF, or seen as the handiwork of the environmental community, it would almost certainly be dead on arrival in the legislature.[15]

"We want to stay at arm's length and come up with independent recommendations," Baker said. He suggested that the governor "convene a

**Fig. 3.2.** Chesapeake Bay Foundation President Will Baker advocated Smart Growth as a way to protect the waters of the Chesapeake Bay. Photo courtesy of the *Baltimore Sun*.

group" to develop recommendations, but to make sure it was not chaired by an environmentalist. He recommended Richard Moe, former chief of staff to Vice President Walter Mondale, who had become president of the Washington, D.C.–based National Trust for Historic Preservation.[16] Baker promised that CBF would build a communications strategy to support the group's recommendations.

"The advocacy group pushes the concept. The government agencies take [the group's recommendations] and put it in a form they can live with. The governor tells the advocacy group to help pass it," he said, explaining how the strategy might work. "As far as our donors are concerned, we have no ownership, but we can put [the recommendations] out and take the heat. All blood, no glory. We can't show the history of how we did it. We can't fight the fight for you if we had more ownership."[17]

He promised "not to try to run a parallel train."

As it turned out, Glendening never appointed the separate group Baker had recommended, but CBF nonetheless maintained its arm's length relationship throughout 1996 and the legislative session of 1997, even as it quietly developed support for Smart Growth. By keeping some distance from Glendening's proposal, CBF was well positioned to press both the administration and the legislature to push the initiative farther than either wanted to go.

Moe, meanwhile, became one of the earliest and most vocal national leaders to praise Maryland's Smart Growth effort. He turned the formerly stodgy National Trust into an activist force for community revitalization, historic preservation, and Smart Growth in Maryland and around the country.

## The "Red Tide" and "Smart Growth"

Once the governor and his staff embarked on the task of developing a growth management initiative, there was never talk of turning back. By mid-May, Glendening was already thinking about how and where he would publicly announce his plans.

About that time, a video produced by a geographic information system (GIS) office at the University of Maryland Baltimore County[18] found its way to the governor's staff offices on the State House second floor. Using satellite imagery, parcel data collected by the Maryland Office of Planning, and other information, the GIS specialists at UMBC had put together a time-lapse animation that depicted the spread of development in Maryland from Colonial times until the present. The date, starting in 1792, was shown in one corner of the screen and spun rapidly through the decades. Meanwhile, development was shown in red dots against a black map. As the years rolled by, the red dots gradually spread outward from major cities and often followed along the straight lines of major roadways. Then, when the year hit 1950, the red dots began to get noticeably thicker and spread rapidly all over the map. By the 1960s, the

**Maps 3.1–5.** Beginning in 1996, Governor Glendening used a series of "Red Tide" maps to demonstrate the spread of development in Maryland over time. In the originals, the parcel data was illustrated in red. Here is an updated version of the "Red Tide" maps created by the Maryland Department of Planning. Here you can see the development patterns in central Maryland beginning with 1929.

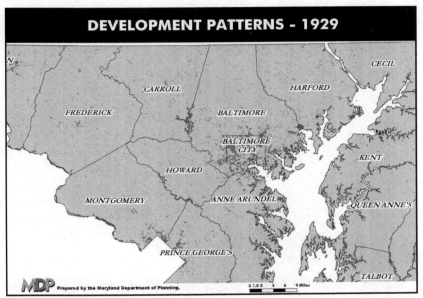

DEVELOPMENT PATTERNS - 1929

Map 3.1

DEVELOPMENT PATTERNS - 1949

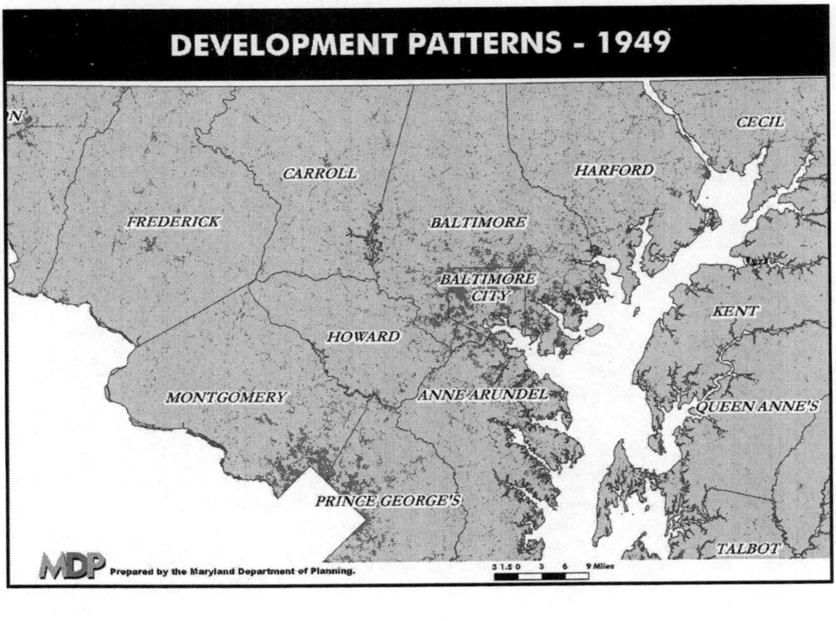

Map 3.2

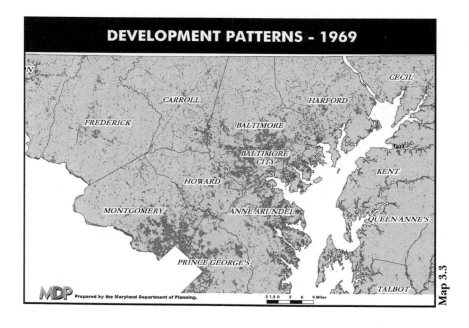

**DEVELOPMENT PATTERNS - 1969**

N

CECIL

CARROLL

HARFORD

FREDERICK

BALTIMORE

BALTIMORE CITY

KENT

HOWARD

MONTGOMERY

ANNE ARUNDEL

QUEEN ANNE'S

PRINCE GEORGE'S

TALBOT

MDP Prepared by the Maryland Department of Planning.

3 1.5 0    3    6    9 Miles

Map 3.3

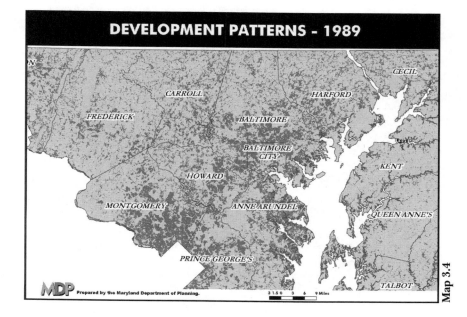

**DEVELOPMENT PATTERNS - 1989**

N

CECIL

CARROLL

HARFORD

FREDERICK

BALTIMORE

BALTIMORE CITY

KENT

HOWARD

MONTGOMERY

ANNE ARUNDEL

QUEEN ANNE'S

PRINCE GEORGE'S

TALBOT

MDP Prepared by the Maryland Department of Planning.

3 1.5 0    3    6    9 Miles

Map 3.4

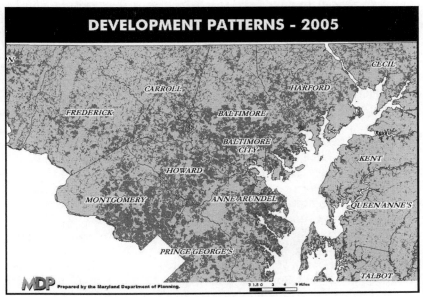

Map 3.5

effect of building the beltways around Baltimore and Washington could be seen; by the '70s, the effect of more interstate highways and the bridge across the Chesapeake Bay at Annapolis; and, by the '80s, the building boom that began to transform much of Maryland.

It was as if someone had dropped a stone in a pond and the ripples just moved outward, except in this case the center of the ponds were Baltimore, Washington, D.C., and, to a lesser extent, places such as Frederick, Cumberland, and Cambridge. It looked like a red tide sweeping over the state, and the staff began referring to it by that name. This was an updated, more sophisticated version of the "measles maps" Kreitner had rolled out during the unsuccessful 1991 campaign to enact the 2020 Commission recommendations.

The governor was entranced. It was exactly what he needed to make his case. The video was accompanied by dramatic music and Glendening immediately understood how powerful it could be in quickly explaining the problem he wanted to address: sprawl development. He could pop the video into a VCR and in just a couple minutes impress upon a doubting legislator or a nervous county commissioner the magnitude of the problem. There it was, right before their eyes: sprawl spreading to every remote corner of the state. How could they dispute it? Never mind that the size of the dots were, by necessity, out of scale with the map and therefore exaggerated the problem. In just minutes, Glendening could explain to almost any audience a trend that reams of statistics failed adequately to convey. As a public relations tool, it was a godsend. (So good was this footage that a few years later Vice President Al Gore used a snippet from the "red tide" tape as part of a longer video he showed when he announced his own national "Livable Communities" initiative.)

The "red tide" video helped the governor and his staff fashion his first public announcement. Certain that the mayors of the state's 154 municipalities* would be likely to support any land use program that meant more state resources for their jurisdictions, the governor decided he would make his first public announcement of his growth management plans at their annual summer meeting. As usual, the Maryland Municipal League conference was scheduled to convene in Ocean City in June. If he could get the mayors on his side early, the governor knew he would succeed in splitting the reaction from local governments. The mayors, he figured, would be with him; but county leaders would be opposed. Once he had buy-in from the mayors, he could then concentrate on getting the counties on board—or at least getting them to modify their resistance or remain neutral. County opposition had killed the 2020 Commission recommendations and Glendening was extremely sensitive to the county threat to his own developing initiative.

Maryland is one of the smallest states in the United States, ranking forty-second in size. But with a population that was 4.7 million in 1990 but projected to grow to 5.3 million by 2000, it ranked as the fifth most densely populated state. And, as the "red tide" slides showed, much of that population was moving out of established cities and towns, such as Baltimore or Cumberland, and into surrounding suburban and exurban counties. This shift reverberated in many of the state's oldest municipalities as the local tax base atrophied, crime increased, basic maintenance became unaffordable, schools declined, and more residents left for—quite literally—greener pastures.

Glendening's strategy for the MML meeting was simply to demonstrate the problem. The governor knew he could not successfully propose a solution until both elected officials and the public understood the dimensions of the problem. The governor and his staff were already thoroughly convinced of the seriousness of the state's development trends. Kreitner, the state planning director, had steadily rolled out the ominous numbers:[19]

- By 2020, there would be more than 650,000 new households in Maryland, many of them likely to be located in the second and third ring suburbs or previously rural land.

*By 2006, there were 157 incorporated municipalities in Maryland.

- The average household size had declined from 3.25 to 2.43, even as lot sizes steadily increased. This meant families were consuming more land to serve fewer people.
- Between 1970 and 1990, more than 420,000 people had moved out of older developed areas, leaving abandoned houses, closed shops, underutilized infrastructure and services, and declining economic prospects in their wake.
- Over the past half-century, Baltimore had become an urban centrifuge, flinging its residents into the surrounding suburbia. A city population that peaked at nearly 1 million in mid-century had plummeted to about 645,000 and was continuing to fall.
- Moreover, as race-inspired "white flight" accelerated, the average family moving out of the city tended to have a salary twice that of any family moving in.
- Because of this dispersed development pattern, the amount of vehicle miles traveled was soaring and projected to rise over the coming decade by an estimated 47 percent. This, of course, put financial pressure on state and local governments alike to build or expand highways.
- Thousands of acres of farmland and forest were being lost every year to development. In just the previous five years, an amount of land four times the size of the proposed Chapman's Landing development had been consumed.
- The infrastructure investments required to keep up with sprawl was costing millions of dollars, perhaps much of it unnecessarily.
- Just driving a child to a school located too far away to walk cost $500 per student per year—money that Kreitner pointed out was then unavailable for classroom use.
- More than $36 million a year was being spent to clean up or fix failed septic systems, yet each year more housing was being built that relied on septic systems.

The face of Maryland was changing, and fast.

About a week before the MML meeting, the *Baltimore Business Journal* broke the story: "Sprawling 'Burbs Next Battlefront?" A subhead read, "Glendening Trying to Whip Up Support."[20] The article focused in part on how the taxes from residential development fell short of covering the cost of local government services for the families that live in those houses. Kreitner, quoted in the article, noted that sprawl was costly to the state as well, citing the expense of building sixty-seven new schools in Montgomery County in the previous twenty years as the county's population migrated from the suburbs adjacent to Washington, D.C., to more rural areas north toward Howard and Frederick counties.

## Setting the Stage for Change

While the governor and his staff may have recognized a problem, it was clear that elected officials and the public at large had not. Some of them may have been concerned about some parts of this overall development picture, but it seemed as if no one—with the possible exception of some of the environmental groups and members of the state's Growth Commission—was looking at the overall picture. Not since the Barnes Commission effort in 1990 and 1991 and the Growth Act of 1992 had anyone dared take a comprehensive view of the growth trends in Maryland and seriously discussed enacting laws that might change them.

To set the stage for such change, the public, elected officials, and even the press had to be convinced there was a problem so serious that a government solution was needed. But those outside the insular world of state government in 1996, especially the press, were focused on many different things, and land use was not one of them.

The big issue that played out that summer was a series of newspaper stories critical of the governor's aggressive campaign fundraising activities. Determined to be amply fortified for a reelection campaign that was still two years away, the governor was beating the bushes for money—and he suffered in the press because of it.

That summer, Governor Glendening also was forced to decide whether a death row inmate should be executed, what to do about the defeat of collective bargaining legislation that he had promised unions he would support, and had to work through tricky political issues surrounding attendance at the national Democratic Convention that summer. Meanwhile, others on the governor's staff were developing their own big legislative programs in anticipation of the 1997 legislative session, including one to provide broader health care coverage for uninsured children, and another to provide state tuition assistance to would-be college students. Each of these initiatives—and the staff behind them—competed for the governor's attention and support.

To convince the mayors meeting in Ocean City on June 24 that land use was a major issue that required state action, the staff convinced the governor to accompany his speech with a showing of the "red tide" video and a computerized Power Point presentation. The idea was to show images that would convey the seriousness of the problem: abandoned buildings, farmland turned into housing developments, traffic congestion, and so on. It may have been the first time in Glendening's career that he accompanied a speech with a Power Point presentation, but it surely would not be the last. Over the next six years, Glendening would give scores of Smart Growth speeches, almost all of them accompanied by Power Point presentations. He and his media staff learned early on that when trying to explain land use issues, pictures and maps and other visual data really helped audiences better understand what was at stake.

In putting together that first Power Point show, the dilemma the governor's press staff faced was that they could not find enough pictures that showed "the problem." Most of the pictures on file or that had been taken by the governor's staff photographers were pictures of the best of Maryland, not the worst. There were plenty of pictures of bucolic, rolling farmland, horse farms with their miles of white fences, brand new traffic interchanges (usually taken at ribbon-cutting ceremonies), shiny new transit cars, or the happy, smiling faces of public officials shaking hand with their equally happy, smiling constituents—the standard "grip and grin" shots that have become the universal currency of politicians. The staff had to dig and search for pictures of buildings with plywood over the windows, or cornfields being turned under by bulldozers, or roads so gridlocked that they appeared to be linear parking lots. It was not hard to find examples of those problems in almost any corner of Maryland, but no one, it seemed, had bothered to take any photographs of them—at least no one in state government. By the time the absence of these pictures was realized, it was almost too late to do anything about it.

Finally, a script was drafted and enough pictures compiled to make the case. The goal: convince the mayors there was a problem and solicit their help in developing a solution. There was no reason to offer any potential solutions so far in advance of the next legislative session, and plenty of reasons not to even try. For one, the governor genuinely did not know in mid-June what he would propose the following January. Moreover, to float trial balloons that early would only give opponents a long lead time to organize their opposition—exactly the problem the Barnes Commission recommendations faced when they were introduced in the General Assembly in 1991.

Finally, it made both practical and political sense to reach out to allies such as the mayors for ideas. If their ideas could get incorporated in the final proposal, they were more likely to help the governor get the measure through.

## The Name "Smart Growth"

With the big speech coming up fast, the workgroup struggled with what to call their new initiative. The Governor's phrase, "Directed Growth," had been expanded to "Directed Growth and Revitalization." Then, on June 6, a new name was chosen: "Neighborhood Conservation and Directed Growth." Two weeks later, on June 18, a final workgroup meeting was held prior to the public announcement at MML. At that meeting, the name was changed again, this time to: "Neighborhood Conservation and Smart Growth."[21]

Six days later, as he stood before the mayors in the low-ceilinged ballroom of the Princess Royale, the beachfront hotel where MML meets each summer, Parris Glendening delivered a speech entitled, "Where Do We Grow from Here?"[22] For the first time in public, he used the phrase, "Smart Growth."

Glendening was not the first person to put those two words together. Others had done so in Maryland and in other states, including "Smart Growth" efforts that dated back at least to the mid-1990s.* While Glendening and his staff did not coin the phrase, what they succeeded in doing was to popularize it.

The phrase "Smart Growth" is now known in almost every state and in planning and land use circles around the world. Academics and advocates of all stripes argue endlessly over what the two words mean and whether it is a good thing or not. No one, however, can dispute that the phrase "Smart Growth" has become a shorthand that summarizes a broad set of issues that includes land use planning, transportation, architecture and design, public health, housing, historic preservation, environmental protection, and more. A computerized Google search for the phrase "Smart Growth" in October 2007 produced 1,720,000 potential responses.

Those who were in the meeting at which "Smart Growth" was picked as the final name for the Maryland land use program have different memories of who said what or who actually proposed the name. The final decision on it, though, was clearly Glendening's.

Stuart Meck, a former senior research fellow at the American Planning Association, traces the use of the phrase "Smart Growth" in a planning or land use context to the use of the word *smart* to describe cutting edge business practices or technology in the mid-1980s. In 1988, for example, Arthur Andersen demonstrated its pioneering sales and inventory tracking technology for retailers at its "Smart Store."

"As with other business concepts, terms, phrases and lingo—such as the phrase 'strategic planning'—the term *smart* gradually seeped into use by self-described progressive nonprofit organizations and government agencies in the nineteen-nineties," Meck said.[23]

Around the same time in 1996 that Maryland was inventing its Smart Growth program, a unit of the U.S. Environmental Protection Agency in Washington—spurred by President Clinton's Council for Sustainable Development—began pulling together a network of organizations interested in this broad set of land use issues and decided to call it the Smart Growth Network.† Harriet Tregoning, who headed that effort within EPA

---

*In 1995, Colorado Governor Roy Romer began a "Smart Growth Initiative" to address traffic congestion, sprawl, and air and water quality concerns. Sprawl Watch. http://www.sprawlwatch.org/colorado.html.

†Maryland became the only state to be invited to join as a partner in the Smart Growth Network, but that was not until late summer of 1997, after Maryland's program had been enacted.

and who was later to serve as both secretary of planning and special secretary for Smart Growth under Glendening during his second term, said the name "Smart Growth" was sparked, in part, by a Smart Growth initiative being advanced by the advocacy group, 1000 Friends of Massachusetts.[24] The American Planning Association later approached Massachusetts for permission to use the phrase "Growing Smart" for its own planning initiative.

The first time the phrase surfaced in the Maryland land use context was probably in the early 1990s after the failure of the Barnes Commission's 2020 recommendations in the General Assembly. It first appeared as part of a green and blue bumper sticker produced by the Maryland Office of Planning that declared: "Grow Smart—Stop Sprawl."

"The bumper sticker was something that was part of our legislation back in ninety-two," said Kreitner, who was the director of the office at the time. "It was just a very simple thing. The Barnes proposal had failed and 'growth management' was a very bureaucratic-sounding name. It made people uncomfortable. And talk about 'planning' was even worse.[25]

"So, my feeling had been that we had to make it a 'cause' out there as opposed to something that was government-sounding. I said, 'If we can get it on a bumper sticker, then we've got something.' So, I worked with our graphics people to come up with this 'Grow Smart—Stop Sprawl' bumper sticker. We would go around giving it out at public meetings. I remember giving one to Parris [Glendening] during his [1994] campaign and he liked it. He said, 'I'm going to put this up.'[26]

"Parris's proposed name, 'Directed Growth,' didn't really have legs. He kind of realized it had a dorky sound to it and was vulnerable to the same attacks as 'Growth Management' in terms of government directing growth. We talked about names that would fly and not be vulnerable to some of these previous criticisms and somehow also reflected the broader tent of interests."[27]

Glendening was especially intent on settling on a name that made clear the program was intended to support existing communities, which is why the word *neighborhood* was included.

During the discussion over the name, Kreitner reported that the Office of Planning bumper sticker had been broadly distributed yet seemed somewhat immune from political attack. "It had some simplicity to it in the sense of saying that we had to do things better—that we could come up with a better way to handle growth," he later explained. "It didn't have a specific connotation that could be troublesome."[28]

Kreitner recalled that when he first used the program's new name on House Speaker Cas Taylor, the powerful Western Maryland legislator asked, "Does it mean that everything that isn't 'Smart Growth' is 'Dumb Growth'?" Kreitner said he let the comment pass without reply, but thought to himself, "Well, okay! Now we're making progress."[29]

While the phrase was approved for use in the governor's Maryland Municipal League speech, a final decision that "Smart Growth" would be part of the initiative's name was still some months away.

"I think it took Parris awhile to be comfortable with it," Kreitner said. "From a political standpoint, he was more sensitive to it than anybody else, wondering, 'How could this be used against me?' Or, 'How could it be attacked?'"[30]

The governor's chief legislative officer was a young lawyer named Steven B. Larsen, whose job it would be to sell the new land use initiative to the General Assembly. "Even after [the name] was floated, I don't think everybody said immediately, 'This is what we're going to do.'" Larsen remembered. "It survived the nitpicking and second-guessing internally. I think a point came where we needed to call it something, and this was the best option that had been floated."[31]

From the legislative standpoint, Larsen found the catchy name to be helpful. "I think the idea of having a program that could be boiled down to a concept that we could articulate was very helpful. Once you explained to people all the things it encompassed, it was helpful to have a shorthand phrase that when you said it, people would say, 'Oh, yeah, that means we're redirecting resources.' Remember, it encompassed budget issues, environmental issues, and revitalization issues—overlapping, but different concepts wrapped up into two words. That was nice. That was helpful."[32]

## "Two Separate Societies"

In his speech to the Municipal League in Ocean City, the governor recalled visiting various cities and towns and walking the streets with various mayors. "From Baltimore City to the Eastern Shore, from the Washington suburbs to Western Maryland, we walked together, seeing the physical signs of the problems we face: boarded up houses, vacant storefronts, closed businesses and urban and rural decay. Likewise, we have watched the steady disappearance of our forest and farmlands.

"I am convinced we have the ability to make things better," he said. "The answer largely depends on how well local governments manage growth, how well we use existing infrastructure, how well we conserve and reinvigorate our existing neighborhoods, and how often we stretch our imaginations and use our creativity to modernize and use what already exists instead of building something new."[33]

Later in the speech he said: "The challenge we face is creating a Maryland in which people recognize that moving up does not have to mean moving out—moving out of our cities and towns, moving out to suburban sprawl."

Glendening noted that four previous governors had talked about the same problem, but none had solved it. Like Mandel years before, Glendening assured the mayors he was not interested in "stripping away the power of local officials . . ."

In case someone in the audience had missed it the first time, the governor reiterated that the state was not trying to take back the local land use control the state had statutorily conferred on local governments. "I want to make it perfectly clear—I am not interested in overruling local officials. I do not want a state zoning board. I am not interested in usurping local authority.[34]

"I know that when a governor starts talking about coping with growth, people get nervous," Glendening acknowledged as he neared the end of his nine-page speech. But he added: "I want you to be nervous—nervous about what happens if we do not act now [and] to make sure you understand that there are real and damaging consequences if we do not take action now."

Two days later, Glendening followed up the MML speech with an op-ed column in the *Baltimore Sun*[35] in which he said he saw an analogy between the effects of sprawl on society and the words of Judge Otto Kerner about race relations twenty-five years before: "We are creating two separate societies, one rich, the other poor; one with good jobs, the other that cannot find work; one in huge houses with perfectly manicured lawns, the other in run-down decaying neighborhoods."

But, for the third time in three days, the governor again bowed to political reality, writing in the *Sun*: "I want to be clear. My administration will not override local zoning boards or create a state zoning board. I will not usurp local authority."[36]

# Chapter 4

# The Initiative Begins to Take Shape

Parris Glendening always operated on a political calendar that essentially shut down each year from mid-June through Labor Day, perhaps the result of the academic calendar he followed during twenty-seven years as a political science professor at the University of Maryland. It was not that he didn't work during those hot summer months, but he usually shied away from public events during that period each year. The public, he always said, wasn't tuned in; they wouldn't be listening. They would be on vacation and disinterested in—or even annoyed by—political pronouncements that might intrude on their blissful week at the beach.

Once his MML speech in June was over and he had given the public fair warning of his intention to develop a land use proposal in time for the 1997 legislative session, the governor retreated from public events at which he might be asked to explain the details of what he intended to do. Instead, he and his staff spent the dog days of that summer trying to figure out the answer to that question.

From the staff perspective, the Smart Growth effort was gaining momentum, drawing in more players from different agencies, and resulting in more meetings, more memos, more work. The two staff members who were trying to keep the workgroup on track were Larsen, the governor's chief legislative lobbyist, and Frece, who headed his press office. Increasingly, however, they were finding they did not have time to oversee the many meetings and issues arising from the Smart Growth effort and meet their other varied responsibilities as well. Running into each other in the marble-walled hallway outside of Room 217 one afternoon shortly before the MML speech, Frece and Larsen agreed the issue was getting so cumbersome and time-consuming that they needed to prevail upon the governor to designate a single point person for Smart Growth.

Around the same time, Ron Young, the former Frederick mayor, was unceremoniously transferred out of his job as deputy secretary of Natural

**Fig. 4.1.** Deputy State Planning Director Ronald N. Young spoke to hundreds of audiences about the state's Smart Growth program. Photo courtesy of the *Baltimore Sun*.

Resources to the deputy director's position at the Office of Planning. This was not intended as a reflection on Young's work or value. Rather, the transfer was for a more pragmatic reason: the governor wanted to move someone off his State House staff and had to find a sufficiently important position for the aide to assume. Young became expendable, or at least transferable. Unfortunately, Young learned of his new assignment from the newspapers. Both Frece and Larsen sensed an opportunity: if the governor would make Young his point person on Smart Growth, it would remove some of the responsibility for the Smart Growth proposal from Frece's and Larsen's shoulders, would allow Young to save face after his sudden transfer to Planning, and would put in charge of the Smart Growth effort someone brimming with ideas and enthusiasm. The governor agreed.

"Neighborhood Conservation and Smart Growth are important goals of this administration. And we are already taking action," Glendening told the mayors in his summer MML speech. He announced that he had formed a sub-cabinet group headed by one of their own, former mayor Ron Young, to "work on a Neighborhood Conservation and Smart Growth initiative."[1]

"The group will identify opportunities for redirecting state agency resources and programs in ways that will foster growth in areas where we all believe it should occur, and away from areas we all believe should be protected," he said. "The group will also consider policy changes and ways to improve the coordination and delivery of state agency services and will suggest possible legislation for introduction during the next session of the General Assembly."[2]

## "We Asked, You Proposed"

Young was put in charge of outreach for the Smart Growth initiative. It was his job to meet with various groups to find out what they thought should be done about the state's land use issues. More specifically, he was to find out what various groups thought the governor should propose or—equally important—*not* propose. He embarked on this task with flair, energy, and an unusual approach.

Young and his staff started by visiting all kinds of groups—community and housing associations, businesses, environmental organizations, farm groups, land trusts, planners and design groups, local governments, and others. Each time, Young and his staff would ask the groups to make specific recommendations "that would prevent sprawl and would make neighborhoods more livable."[3] They collected every major recommendation, then classified the various recommendations in one of three categories: Administrative, Legislative, and Other. The resulting booklet grew to 101 pages.

Young's unusual twist was that he took this new book of recommendations and sent it back to all the same groups so each could see and comment upon the ideas of others. He titled the book: "We Asked, You

Proposed: Now We Need Your Recommendations." From the staff's perspective, the idea was to winnow out the recommendations that were either too extreme or too weak to have any chance of gaining consensus support. It also was intended to remove some of the fear that had set in among those who felt they had been kept in the dark back in 1990 as the 2020 Commission fashioned its recommendations. Young knew that rumors or speculation about what the administration might propose could be more damaging to their effort than the actual proposals. Besides, there weren't any actual proposals yet and part of his task was to assure nervous local government officials as well as environmentalists and others that no final decisions had been made and that it was not too late for them to weigh in.

To reassure any of the recipients of the "We Asked, You Proposed" booklet who were unnerved by the very idea of the state involving itself more deeply in land use issues, the booklet carried a disclaimer stripped across the bottom of *every* page that read: "These suggestions were recommended by fellow Marylanders. They have not been endorsed, supported or adopted by the Administration."

As the ideas poured in, Young and his staff categorized them as "very strongly supported," "strongly supported," "supported," "mild support," "split opinion," and "oppose[d]." Financial incentives for businesses in revitalization areas, planning assistance grants, police residency incentives, restrictions on transportation funding, and use of state-owned surplus property to foster economic growth and private investment were all listed as "very strongly supported."

Measures to broaden the state's Forest Conservation Act, its Endangered Species Conservation Act, or to strengthen the powers of "home rule" counties all received "split opinions." A deceptively small number of proposals were listed as "opposed," perhaps because stakeholders were worried about offending the governor. One idea listed under "split opinions or little interest" was the notion of establishing flexible environmental standards that would vary from urban to suburban to rural areas.

## The Legislative Package Takes Shape

Based in part on Young's outreach efforts and in part on the internal meetings of the workgroup, the broad outline of the Smart Growth initiative began to take form by early September. Jim Brady, the governor's narrowly focused and sometimes mutinous economic development secretary, demanded that the package include brownfields legislation, saying the issue had become "bigger than life" to the business community. "There has to be a bill the administration is clearly behind," he strongly advised.[4]

On September 10, the workgroup began to list the elements that might make up a Smart Growth legislative package for January:[5]

1.  The first and most obvious item was a brownfields bill. Disputes between the business and environmental communities over details of the bill remained, but there was no dispute over whether brownfields legislation would be included as part of the Smart Growth package. Larsen, who was in charge of bringing the warring sides together, was optimistic passage was possible, though he said it was unlikely to reach agreement until the legislative session was underway and pressure built on both sides to reach a compromise.

2.  The second idea would be much more contentious. It was a new concept developed by the workgroup called "Priority Urban Service Boundaries," which would delineate areas that would be eligible for future state financial assistance for growth. Areas not within these boundaries would, for the first time, not be eligible for such assistance. The part that made the concept contentious was a plan to have the state, rather than local governments, set the criteria for how the boundaries would be drawn. Beyond being a recommendation of the staff, that shift in authority also would fulfill a promise the governor had made to CBF's Will Baker.

3.  While much of the focus remained on mechanisms to stimulate revitalization in older communities, some workgroup members also advanced the idea of using the proceeds from the sale of state bonds to pay for farmland and natural resource preservation. This would mean that cash-strapped land preservation programs would suddenly have access to millions of dollars more.

4.  Copying a concept used in several Pennsylvania cities, the workgroup proposed enabling legislation that would permit local governments to enact a split property tax rate, with different rates assigned for each piece of land and the improvements on that land. The idea was that development could be promoted in certain areas by keeping the tax rate high on land, but low on buildings. This way, owners who developed their properties would not be penalized by having to pay sharply higher taxes, nor would they gain much by keeping lands vacant that were suitable for redevelopment.

5.  One of the most active and innovative strategists in the workgroup was Ellen Janes, a soft-spoken but politically attuned Baltimorean who focused on revitalization issues for the Department of Housing and Community Development. One of her contributions to this initial package of ideas was the notion of starting a small pilot program called Live Near Your Work. The goal was to offer tax benefits to encourage

employees to buy houses closer to where they worked. This, in turn, would cut down on long distance commuting, take greater advantage of infrastructure or service investments, and help rebuild downtrodden neighborhoods.

6. Just as the brownfields legislation was designed to draw business support for the Smart Growth package, or using bond proceeds for land preservation would attract environmental or agricultural industry support, other elements of the program were targeted to other major stakeholders. The Maryland Municipal League, for example, wanted the state to grant targeted tax relief to encourage business and residential development in older areas. The concept was added to the September 10 list, but the details were yet to be worked out.

7. Similarly, the mayors wanted the state to approve legislation that would make municipal incorporation easier. It was added to the list, but dropped off the agenda not long afterward. It represented a political fight between the municipalities and the counties and the State House staff saw no advantage of thrusting the governor into the middle of that dispute.

8. Home builders and some officials within the Maryland Association of Counties voiced support for a concept of trading development rights from protected lands to lands designated for growth. So, the idea of adding a Transferable Development Rights (TDR) bill to the package made the list.

9. An idea attributed to a single legislator, Delegate Joan Pitkin from Glendening's home county of Prince George's, also made the initial list. It was to establish "telecommuting workforce centers" around the state to make it easier for Marylanders to work long-distance by computer rather than driving long distance to their offices.

10. In 1991, Maryland's General Assembly had enacted a Forest Conservation Act to require developers to replace some of the trees cleared for new development. Despite broad support for the concept, the program was not working very smoothly, so builders and others pushed to incorporate corrective legislation as part of the Smart Growth package.

11. One of the most controversial ideas emanated from Young and others at the Office of Planning who were concerned that much of the sprawl development occurring in the state relied on septic systems rather than public sewers. If the state could control the rate of development on septic systems by charging

a tax or higher fee for septics than for sewer, they reasoned, then the state might be able to constrain sprawl development.

12. The final item in the September 10 list was a renewed attempt to have the governor revise and issue a Smart Growth executive order that would require that state facilities be located in designated areas consistent with the Smart Growth concept.

After five months of meetings, both internally and with outside groups, the Smart Growth initiative was finally beginning to take shape.

# Chapter 5

# The Inside/Outside Strategy

Back in 1978, some eighteen years before people starting using the phrase "Smart Growth," a former state transportation secretary named Harry R. Hughes was elected governor in one of the biggest political upsets in Maryland history. His running mate was an obscure Prince George's County councilman named Samuel W. Bogley III. When Lieutenant Governor Bogley moved into his new office on the second floor of the Maryland State House in early 1979, he brought with him a young aide named John R. Griffin. Bogley was subsequently dumped from Hughes's reelection ticket in 1982, but Griffin stayed on, moving over to the governor's staff.

In 1984, Griffin, Verna Harrison, and other staffers helped Hughes develop and push to passage a landmark package of legislation to protect the Chesapeake Bay. Once enacted, Griffin and Harrison were transferred from the State House to the Department of Natural Resources, where they became secretary Torrey C. Brown's righthand assistants in implementing the new bay protection laws. In late winter 1995, after twelve years as secretary, Glendening asked Brown to leave and named Griffin to succeed him.

Burly, gregarious, confident, Griffin was totally immersed in natural resources issues. He traveled the state, meeting with watermen, hunters, animal advocacy groups, recreational fishermen, kayakers, farmers, and others. He toured state parks, listened to the concerns of DNR police, and promoted the use of state-owned natural resource recreation areas for "eco-tourism." He and his staff became the regional leaders on Chesapeake Bay protection and, in doing so, became nationally recognized experts in watershed protection. He worked hard to keep the morale at DNR high.

Griffin developed frank working relationships with the top people at the Chesapeake Bay Foundation and other environmental groups, and brought together a new group of business leaders who had a special affinity for hunting, fishing, or other outdoor activities. He called them the "Outdoor Caucus."

**Fig. 5.1.** Natural Resources Secretary John R. Griffin (left), here with Agricultural Secretary Lewis Riley (center) and state Delegate Norm Conway, pushed hard in 1996 to have the Rural Legacy concept merged with Glendening's emerging Smart Growth initiative. Photo courtesy of the *Baltimore Sun*.

"I pretty much handpicked them," Griffin recalled. "I formed that group principally because I wanted to get influence from people in the private sector who loved the outdoors—to get them to be more aligned with us, to get their views and, indeed when we were aligned, to be quiet advocates for natural resources."[1]

Griffin also forged relationships with national environmental and land preservation organizations, from the Isaac Walton League to the American Farmland Trust to the National Land Trust Alliance. When Griffin wasn't meeting with these groups, he was often on the phone with their leaders, sounding them out about ideas, trying to convince them to support new approaches, ironing out messy disputes. DNR employees became accustomed to seeing Griffin at almost any time of morning or evening sitting in his big SUV in the DNR parking lot, just returned from or already late for a meeting, talking on his cell phone to one group or another, puffing on a fat cigar and often running a brush through his long wavy hair. Griffin was popular with his staff and his candid style gained him respect even from those who disagreed with him or his department's positions. But his cowboy style grated on the more professorial Glendening and their relationship, even at the best of times, was strained.

Over the years, Griffin developed an intimate working relationship with a small group of men and women with the capacity to think about natural resources issues in more global terms. They would play out the "what if?" scenarios—What if we insisted that tree-lined buffers be maintained or planted along all rivers and streams? What if we got business leaders to understand the benefits to their companies and their employees of protecting wilderness areas, or the state's abundant natural beauty? What if we could find a way to put more public money behind protecting the best remaining lands in the state?

The makeup of this informal group varied over the years, but it grew to include Mike Nelson, a good-natured veteran of state government who headed DNR's capital projects division, Verna Harrison, a detail-oriented professional who had moved from the State House to DNR with Griffin, Ford Rowan, a former TV anchorman turned conservationist, Calman J. "Buddy" Zamoiski, a Baltimore businessman influential in political circles, Rob Deford, the owner of Maryland-based Bordy Vineyards, Bill Eichbaum, a former head of environmental health regulations for the state of Maryland who had since moved to become a vice president at the World Wildlife Fund, and two phenomenal men who headed an Arlington, Virginia–based, nonprofit land preservation outfit called The Conservation Fund. One was the fund's vice president, an articulate, Alabama-raised lawyer and writer named Ed McMahon, and the other was its energetic president and founder, Patrick Noonan. Members of this informal group would run into each other at public events or congregate over beer on outings with Griffin's "Outdoor Caucus" or over dinner in Washington restaurants. Together, over time, they would strategize about the science, politics, and financial realities of natural resource protection.

They began to form a consensus that the land preservation programs then in effect simply weren't working. There wasn't enough money to do the job, there wasn't enough public understanding of the threat, and there often was no comprehensive plan to guide which lands should be protected. Too often the farms or other land that were being protected were isolated from any other protected property, providing little net gain in terms of habitat, water quality, or other environmental protection. Even the continuation of farming, the basic goal of many of these land protection programs, became unachievable as development increasingly fragmented large agricultural areas.

By the fall of 1996, with Governor Glendening moving swiftly to put together his Smart Growth initiative, Griffin and his co-conspirators saw an opportunity to move their land preservation agenda to center stage. The trick, they agreed, was to convince the governor to balance his "inside" strategy for revitalizing older communities with an "outside" strategy to protect rural resource lands threatened by sprawling development.

By then, Griffin had been working on this concept for nearly two years. He talked about the idea publicly for the first time at the Tidewater Inn in Easton at the first meeting of the Eastern Shore Land Conservancy, which was headed by Griffin's mentor, former governor Hughes. Some months before, Griffin had quietly convened a group of technical experts and state agency representatives[2] to explore the idea of a joint agricultural and natural resource habitat protection program for a several counties area of the Upper Eastern Shore renowned for its rich soil and known as the "Agriculture Security Corridor." The idea was to authorize $25 million to $30 million in revenue bonds to protect farmland in the corridor as a pilot program that, if successful, could be extended statewide.[3]

H. Grant Dehart, who oversaw land preservation programs on Griffin's staff at DNR, recalled how Griffin wanted to team with Secretary of Agriculture Lewis Riley to pool land preservation resources to protect lands that featured multiple resources, both agricultural and natural habitats.[4] Riley, a farmer from the Lower Eastern Shore, was friendly with Griffin and sympathetic to the task. The idea was to finance a little bit each year until the entire Agriculture Security Corridor was protected. At an earlier DNR staff retreat, Dehart and others had discussed with the secretary a new national land protection program sponsored by The Nature Conservancy called "The Last Great Places" initiative. Griffin started thinking about a "Maryland's Greatest Places" initiative.

"That was sort of my take on it," Griffin recalled. "We needed to evaluate the areas of the state that still had the best combination of rural landscapes and natural resources, that could be preserved and were susceptible to that, and to try to allocate funding over time to get the job done—not this sporadic thing we had been doing."[5]

On September 11, 1996, Griffin sent Glendening a four-page letter marked "Confidential" at the top.[6] It opened by reminding the governor that when he first saw the "red tide" video he reacted by asking, "'How many more farms and forests will be lost to sprawl by the year 2020?'"

Griffin seized on that image. "When the countryside or greenbelt that surrounds a community begins to disappear, the loss of 'sense of place' strikes an emotional chord. . . . This is what people care about. Saving these places is the most powerful reason for people to support your smart growth initiative," he argued.[7]

"The strategies associated with revitalizing existing growth areas, which has thus far been the crux of your smart growth initiative, lay an important foundation for the future . . . the long term future! Neither you as governor, nor the public, will witness the success of these initiatives on the ground for years and years to come. Meanwhile, as the state works to turn urban areas around, the countryside will proceed to fall victim to unbridled development. The results," Griffin wrote, "will be a visible reminder that sprawl is continuing to control our state's destiny."[8]

Then he rolled out his proposal: "A perfect complement to your investments in neighborhood conservation is to make the preservation of Maryland's farms and forests a much more prominent element of your overall smart growth initiative. Before the end of your first term, (at a cost substantially lower than the aggregate cost of your other growth initiatives), we can put in place the tools and resources to begin immediately to preserve this 'green infrastructure,' the loss of which represents the most compelling reason for smarter growth."[9]

Griffin's strategy was to appeal to Glendening's political ambition by positioning the proposal as a way Glendening could personally "create an environmental legacy of tens of thousands of 'green' acres saved from development.[10]

"Governor, time is of the essence," he said. "When key parcels are threatened by development, it is often the case that they are lost before funds are available on a [pay-as-you-go] basis."[11] He added that using bonds to pay for land preservation could be more cost effective than the state's existing and much slower pay-as-you-go program because the interest rate paid on bonds was often lower than the appreciation rate for land that usually took several years to buy.

He proposed a two-phase program that would begin with a pilot project to purchase conservation easements in two focus areas, one on either side of the Chesapeake Bay. "These areas would reflect a confluence of prime forest land, agribusiness, rural villages, and wildlife habitat, key components of Maryland's countryside," the DNR secretary wrote.[12] He suggested using a small portion of the state's existing parkland acquisition program, called Program Open Space, to provide the funding that would jump start this new land acquisition initiative. To bolster his case, Griffin convinced former governor Hughes to stop by to see Glendening and advocate for the program. Hughes was on good terms with the new governor, had endorsed him when Glendening was a candidate, and was widely seen as a leading voice for protection of the Chesapeake Bay. Griffin said later he believed the visit helped convince Glendening.[13]

In his memo, Griffin proposed that the governor simultaneously announce his intention to expand the state's land preservation program over the next five years, but acknowledged the success of the effort would depend on public support. "Using a sophisticated public outreach and marketing strategy, you will galvanize public support for accelerating our land conservation efforts before it is too late," he recommended.[14]

He summarized the concept by saying, "Governor, a multi-year effort to directly protect Maryland's green infrastructure is the perfect complement to the many initiatives needed to make our older communities more livable. Although this strategy will not solve all growth management problems, it provides your administration with the opportunity to make a mark on the countryside that is highly visible, emotionally appealing, and a lasting legacy."[15]

The feedback from the State House was swift and positive, Dehart recalled. "The governor thought it was a great idea, but that it needed to be statewide, not a pilot. He wanted to go with it full-bore and do it with as much money as he could get, and do it all over the state."[16]

# Chapter 6

# "The Most Important Thing
in the Whole Administration"

Despite staff enthusiasm for the developing Smart Growth project, the Glendening administration as a whole was suffering and the governor's personal popularity was plummeting. The still-new administration staff was being dragged relentlessly down by a seemingly endless string of critical news reports about the governor's political problems, about his fundraising, and about potential challengers who saw the new governor as vulnerable. For the staff, the emerging Smart Growth initiative was a tonic, a welcome distraction.

Members of the workgroup knew they were onto something. They were having fun being creative and making connections between seemingly unrelated issues and ideas. Just as Griffin had hit on the big-picture linkage between urban revitalization and rural preservation, others on the workgroup were trying to identify just as provocative, if less sweeping, linkages between other components of the program.

If Ellen Janes's Live Near Your Work program were to curtail long-distance commuting, might that not have a small but beneficial effect on reducing air pollution? If Ron Young's idea to let police officers take their squad cars home at night was implemented, could the simple presence of police cars in residential neighborhoods help discourage crime? Would not the brownfields cleanup legislation being pushed by Jim Brady and Jim Fielder inevitably lead to redevelopment, which in turn would produce more inner city jobs, which would then lead to reductions in social welfare and even criminal justice costs? The staff began to realize that everywhere they looked the knee bone seemed to be connected to the thigh bone.

What the program needed, however, was a central unifying theme. One morning early that fall, Nishida, Larsen, and Frece met in a small

**Fig. 6.1.** As secretary of the environment, Jane Nishida was at the center of the dispute between environmentalists and the business community over the brownfields' cleanup legislation. Photo courtesy of the *Baltimore Sun.*

conference room on the top floor of the Department of Business and Economic Development headquarters in Baltimore for the express purpose of hammering out a theme that would sum up what Smart Growth was trying to achieve. It would be a way the governor and everyone on the staff could begin talking about the initiative. This would be "the message."

Gradually, three interconnected goals began to emerge: Smart Growth would enhance the state's older communities; it would protect its best remaining farms and natural areas from sprawl; and it would save taxpayers from the high cost of building infrastructure to support far-flung development. Urban; rural; fiscally prudent.

While the details of the new program still had not been decided or announced, staff began talking to outside groups in these general terms. The reaction ranged from nervousness among county leaders to exhilaration among environmentalists.

On September 11, 1996, Sandy Hillyer, an environmental consultant from Annapolis, sent Frece an unsolicited memorandum that presciently outlined the opportunities Glendening was creating for Maryland, both programmatically and for the governor politically. The tall, redheaded Hillyer had played a key role in the 1994 defeat of Disney's efforts to build a major American history theme park on three thousand acres of rolling horse country near the Manassas Civil War battlefield in piedmont Virginia and was attuned to the politics of land use in the region.

Noting the "three legs that support the work now underway: resource protection, urban revitalization, and fiscal efficiency," Hillyer said, "I would add economic development as a fourth, and overarching objective. A directed development agenda will further economic development directly by clarifying where developers and businesses should make their investments, removing barriers to developing there, expediting permit reviews and fostering certainty. Businesses thinking of locating in Maryland will also be encouraged by assurance that areas deemed appropriate for development will be supported by timely investments in infrastructure. Indirectly, a state that achieves a high degree of resource protection, urban revitalization, and fiscal efficiency will also provide a high quality of life, which will make it easier for businesses to recruit skilled workers."[1]

Hillyer, an ardent environmentalist, went on to recommend that the developing Smart Growth initiative be positioned as "boastfully pro-development." It "should in part be prompted on the basis of its promise for creating jobs [and] it should be distinguished from the obsolete 'pro-business' posture associated with across the board tax cuts, deregulation, and a laissez-faire attitude towards patterns of development." Using arguments that Glendening and his aides would use for years to come in making the case for Smart Growth, Hillyer added, "This attitude ultimately burdens society, including businesses, with higher costs, clogged transportation systems, crowded schools, loss of resource lands, air and water pollution and isolation of an economic and racial underclass in expanding urban ghettos."[2]

Maryland's greatest opportunity for a breakthrough lay in the leadership potential from Glendening, Hillyer said. "He understands the issues as well as any governor in the country." But such change, he said, could not be brought about in a single year.

"A long term campaign is needed that bridges Governor Glendening's first and second terms and that integrates policy initiatives with a far-reaching political strategy. This campaign must build from year to year, using building blocks to achieve piecemeal what could never be achieved by a single stroke, or in a single session of the General Assembly, or even the Governor's first term."[3]

Based on his experience working in other states, Hillyer warned that the task would be difficult. "In spite of its destructiveness, sprawl is the reigning monarch in Maryland, as it is in most of metropolitan America. Acting on their own, the best efforts of separate interest groups, including the business community as well as environmentalists, will ultimately succeed only in perpetuating the status quo. However, with strong political leadership, it is possible to pull together a broad-based sustainable development coalition capable of turning the tide."[4]

Years later, it is uncertain whether Glendening ever saw or read Hillyer's memorandum, but the approaches he outlined and the arguments he made were the approaches and arguments Glendening and his staff would later adopt as their own.

## A Change of Culture

On a beautiful fall morning toward the end of September 1996, twenty-three members of Glendening's top staff drove their cars across the Chesapeake Bay Bridge and south on U.S. Route 50 to a cabin at Wye Island, a 2,450-acre wildlife management area in Talbot County managed by the DNR Park Service. Attending this Smart Growth staff retreat were six cabinet secretaries, including the governor's budget and transportation secretaries, the deputy secretaries of two other departments, the director and deputy director of the Office of Planning, and the governor's communications director and his press secretary.

Young, the deputy secretary at planning, set the tone. "This," he said, "may be the most important thing done in the whole administration."[5]

The purpose of the retreat was to go over the results of the "We Asked, You Proposed" survey and put together a formal recommendation for the governor. The outreach effort, Young reported, "was really well received. Everybody saw everything." But he suggested the biggest obstacle may be internal, not external. "The most resistance," he said, "is from the departments in the state, not from the public."[6]

For more than six hours, the group discussed various concepts, trying to envision how they could be implemented, whether they would have the desired effect, and what the financial or political cost of each would be. Gradually, many in the group realized that success in this endeavor might depend on a fundamental change in thinking, both inside and outside of government.

"What we need is a culture change," said Frederick W. Puddester, the secretary of budget and management. Griffin agreed: "If we don't change the way we behave, we're just kidding ourselves."[7]

## Priority Funding Areas

A week later, the workgroup met again with Glendening and agreed upon the central element of the Smart Growth approach: the designation of specific growth areas in every county that would be the only areas eligible for future state financial assistance for growth. They would be called "Priority Funding Areas" because—quite obviously—they were to be areas that would receive top priority for state funding.[8] (In subsequent years, Glendening intentionally avoided using this bureaucratic sounding name in speeches, opting instead for the more informal, less precise language of "Smart Growth Areas.")

The governor said he wanted every local government to have a defined growth boundary, that he wanted the boundaries to be drawn based on a set of state (rather than local) criteria, and vowed that the state would assist with growth projects only within the boundaries and that "anything outside, they are on their own."[9]

This would be a departure from past practice. The Smart Growth approach was to limit by geography or location where the state would support new growth and where it would not. Although provisions in the '92 Growth Act moved the state in this direction, it does not appear those provisions were ever rigorously enforced. Up until this time, if a project was otherwise eligible for state financial assistance, no one asked the question: "Where is it located?" No one asked whether a new shopping mall might hurt an older downtown business district, or if a new housing development might so fragment farmland as to make it unworkable, or so destroy forests that natural habitats for interior songbirds or other animals might be lost forever. No one had ever questioned whether the state's support of growth on the fringe might conflict with other state goals for the economic well-being of older towns and cities. Almost any new highway project was seen as "progress" and almost any new development as "expanded tax base."

The "Priority Funding Area" concept represented a new way of thinking, what might be called governmental multitasking. The idea was that the net result of governmental action should be the simultaneous accomplishment of multiple policy objectives, not just individual or departmental goals. Rather than seek projects that met economic development goals without regard to environmental effects, or that sought to protect the environment without regard to adverse effects on business, the idea was to find ways to meet these and other goals with the same action. This approach would later highlight the inherent and unavoidable conflicts of certain policy goals, but nevertheless would become the heart of the Maryland Smart Growth initiative.

A policy wonk at heart, Glendening's enthusiasm grew. He began talking about possibly holding a fall environmental conference, about visits to designated "wildlands" areas around the state, about a "no net loss" wetlands protection strategy, about expanding by miles the effort to preserve or grow forested buffers along the banks of streams and rivers, and about accelerating the rate of farmland preservation. In almost every other area of his political life he was being pilloried. He sensed opportunity here. Internally, he told his top aides, "We need to redefine ourselves."[10] But could he accomplish that with Smart Growth? With a land use program? His political consultants expressed their doubts.

As the legislative session drew closer, edgy interest groups demanded to know what the governor intended to propose. Young and his Office of Planning assistant Tom Bass had met with seemingly everyone to talk about the governor's plans, but always only in generalities. Increasingly, the interest groups demanded the details. Even as late as mid-October, however, the final details had not been decided. Moreover, Glendening was extremely cautious about the timing of the release of any details. Do it too early and the forces against change will have time to prepare their attack. Do it too late and legislators will complain they did not have sufficient time to consider the proposal and will, at best, postpone any decision until they can complete "a summer study"—the graveyard for many good legislative ideas.

"Do not say anything until we confer," Glendening instructed fifteen members of his staff at the second of two long workgroup meetings held October 16, adding, "We need to build a constituency for it first."[11] But that put Young and others on the staff in a bind. How could they build a constituency for it if they couldn't tell the potential constituency any details about what the administration intended to propose? Young especially was in a squeeze. As a former mayor, county officials were already suspicious of him, seeing him as more aligned with the municipal point of view. When he demurred when pressed for details, county officials thought he was hiding some devilish plan because he knew the counties would hate it. Young knew, however, that if he said too much and it got back to the State House, he would then be in trouble with the governor. More worrisome, it could sabotage the whole effort.

Still, he was optimistic. "Interest in this subject has never been this high," Young said. "We have an opportunity to seize something. A lot of these items [discussed as possible components of the program] are easy to do."[12]

The governor said he liked the idea of "Priority Service Areas," but wanted the name changed. Environment Secretary Jane Nishida, who often had the governor's ear, said it would be a "mistake" to let the local governments determine the boundaries of the growth areas. "We need to come up with the criteria," she recommended.[13]

Similarly, the governor said he would support "a significant expansion of funding for ag[ricultural] easements" as well as Griffin's proposed Rural Legacy program. But, of the latter, he said, "Change the name."[14]

The housing department's Ellen Janes and others in the workgroup began pushing a new idea they felt was necessary to make redevelopment projects in older communities realistically possible: an "Infrastructure Fund." By pooling funds from the Departments of Transportation, Business and Economic Development, Housing and Community Development, and Natural Resources, the Janes group felt the governor could propose to put as much as $26 million in a fund to be used for low interest loans and grants to redevelopment areas.[15]

But the idea was controversial within the staff. Some on the workgroup felt $26 million was not nearly enough to do the job and suggested so small a fund might actually give the governor's critics a chance to ridicule him for just giving "lip service" to the idea. In a year in which the governor was likely to have only a small, if any, budget surplus with which to grease the machinery of government, others saw a political "opportunity cost" of using $26 million for sewer and water lines and other mundane infrastructure improvements for which they were certain the public would give the governor zero credit. Even Glendening himself told his staff at one point that fall that if there was any extra revenue to be spent in the FY 98 budget that was then being prepared, it would be put into public education. His instructions regarding the cost of the new Smart Growth program were clear: Do it within existing resources; it was not to be a big new spending program.

Money or not, Glendening clearly recognized that getting the Smart Growth program passed would be a challenge and began to compare it to the two big, divisive issues that—with gubernatorial power, persuasion, and, of course, money—he succeeded in pushing to passage in the 1996 legislative session: the two stadium projects and the gun control legislation.

"I intend to put the force of this office behind this," Glendening told the workgroup. "This is like the gun bill, and the stadiums."[16]

## Developing Support

A hallmark of Parris Glendening's governing style has always been long-range planning. To use the chess analogy, he is good at seeing the whole board, anticipating his opponent's moves and putting his own pieces in a position to win when the time is right. As the Smart Growth initiative began to take form, Glendening repeatedly returned to the themes of outreach, communication, message, and the need to build constituencies. He named Frece, Griffin, Young, and Senior Counselor Eleanor Carey, a Baltimore lawyer the governor had recruited to his staff in October 1996, to head the outreach effort.

The plan was simply to launch a broad frontal attack. The staff would try to place columns in state and local newspapers, get letters from the governor or cabinet secretaries into organizational newsletters, appear with supporters from the municipalities, and try to arrange TV appearances to talk about the need for Smart Growth. They also would seek the help of influential and sympathetic officials, such as Baltimore County Executive Dutch Ruppersberger, to soften the resistance among county officials, and to enlist the help of those who would likely become the initiative's strongest supporters within the environmental community, such as Montgomery County State Senator Brian Frosh and former Anne Arundel County State Senator Gerald Winegrad.

"The public has to understand that Easton [for example] is where we are favoring jobs and development. Farms two miles outside, we're trying to protect," Glendening told his troops.[17]

Staff members were directed to develop a video illustrating the problems brought on by sprawl development and a booklet of Smart Growth initiatives to be ready in time for the legislative session. Others were dispatched to assure not only the support of the Chesapeake Bay Foundation, but their active help in lining up votes as well. "Talking points" about the linkage between Smart Growth and bay protection were to be drafted and circulated.

To nail down support in Baltimore, members of the workgroup were instructed to meet with the Urban League, the NAACP, and the Legislative Black Caucus to make the case that their constituencies had a major stake in this issue. Briefings for General Assembly leaders and the leadership of the Maryland Association of Counties were to be scheduled.[18] "Legislators are all asking about Smart Growth," Larsen, the governor's chief legislative lobbyist, reported to the workgroup on October 23. Young added, "The levels of expectation are high."[19]

Dianna Rosborough, the governor's press secretary, was still tinkering with the name and crafting parts of the message. She suggested "Maryland Growing Smarter" instead of "Smart Growth." To assure citizen support, she said the administration position should be: "We're not trying to tell anybody they can't do anything. We're trying to do it in a way that preserves the land . . . and saves taxpayers money. Will this stifle growth or development? No, these are not growth limitations."[20]

Kreitner and Young were working on another front. Kreitner quietly provided a $5,000 grant from the Office of Planning to a small group in Baltimore that wanted to set up a pro–Smart Growth "1000 Friends" citizens' group modeled after the 1000 Friends of Oregon and 1000 Friends of Florida. The Abell Foundation, a Baltimore-based nonprofit, also provided seed money to the group.[21]

Kreitner and Young began meeting with Karen Lewand, who represented the Baltimore chapter of the American Institute of Architects, and Al Barry, a professional planner in the city, to encourage them to form "1000 Friends of Maryland."

Barry reported, "We're getting calls daily from groups asking, 'How can we get involved?' People can't escape [from advancing development] anymore." Lewand, however, acknowledged that many of the callers were pessimistic about whether Smart Growth or any other initiative could reverse the state's development trends. "People don't believe [sprawl] can be stopped," she said.[22]

Lewand and Barry recommended the administration enlist the help of Preservation Maryland, the state's historic preservation organization, and try to capture the kind of audience that regularly tunes into the popular Maryland Public Television show, "Outdoors Maryland."

"You need to show what the state will look like in twenty years. What is the real cost? Show graphically the air pollution and other impacts. Get people's attention," Barry suggested. "Get environmentalists and banks to do an independent study of the economic impact of sprawl."[23]

## Rallying the Environmental Army

John Griffin knew the idea of boosting land preservation would be powerful, but the challenge would be to get environmentalists and other supporters to see the value of linking it to community redevelopment. He convinced Governor Glendening to forget for the time being the Chesapeake Bay Foundation and other Maryland-based environmental groups and make his pitch instead to the leaders of an array of national environmental groups and select Maryland business leaders. The strategy was to get these national groups to rally their members as advocates for Smart Growth. Griffin knew the land preservation sell would probably be easy; but to get them also to support the idea of supporting more growth anywhere—even in existing communities—would be hard. He knew the membership of some of these groups would prefer a "no growth" strategy and that the governor faced the task of convincing them that "no growth" was not a realistic option.

At mid-morning on Wednesday, November 6, Governor Glendening welcomed a dozen national environmental leaders to a light brunch at the governor's brick mansion across the street from the State House in Annapolis. Seated around the huge mahogany table in the mansion's formal dining room were Patrick Noonan, president of the Conservation Fund; Ed McMahon, a Conservation Fund vice president and director of the National

Greenways Program; Bill Eichbaum, director of U.S. programs for the World Wildlife Fund; Jean Hocker, president of the National Land Trust Alliance; Nina Rodale Houghton, chairman of the Wye Institute; Ford Rowan, a former NBC newsman and now a principal of a political consulting firm, Rowan and Blewitt, Inc.; Rob Deford of Maryland-based Bordy Vineyards; Baltimore political activist Buddy Zamoiski, chairman of the board of Independent Distributors, Inc.; and Warren Hortenstein, president of Kannegiesser USA. Also present were surrogates for Richard Moe, president of the National Trust for Historic Preservation, Ralph Grossi, the president of the American Farmland Trust; and Paul Hansen, president of the National Isaac Walton League.[24]

Noonan, Eichbaum, Houghton, Rowan, Deford, Zamoiski, and Hortenstein were all members of Griffin's "DNR Outdoor Caucus," business leaders who liked outdoor activities and who met with top DNR leaders about four times a year to brainstorm issues related to DNR projects. The brunch had been completely arranged by Griffin.

Glendening sat in the center of one long side of the table. Joining him were three members of his staff (Carey, Larsen, and Frece) and the secretaries or deputy secretaries of five departments: Griffin, Agriculture Secretary Lewis Riley, Planning Director Kreitner and his deputy, Young, Environment Secretary Nishida, and General Services Secretary Gene Lynch.

Glendening's agenda was to convince these leaders to get their organizations excited about Smart Growth broadly, build public support for the legislation and put up some money to do public opinion polling and possibly advertising.

"I'm absolutely committed to this," Glendening said after describing the two-pronged revitalization/land preservation framework of the still evolving Smart Growth initiative. "I know we're not talking about an overnight solution, but clearly this is the time for decisive action. We're looking at both sides of the equation—open space and to reinvigorate our older communities." Reflecting momentarily on the current state of affairs, the governor said, "If you try to devise a system that is the most wasteful of dollars, we did it."[25]

There was a momentary pause and then Eichbaum, who had headed the state's environmental regulatory efforts under Governor Hughes, was the first of the invited guests to respond. "We see the model in Maryland," he said. "It is very innovative and important. I'm committed to working to make it happen."[26]

Then the discussion slowly moved around the table, with each of the guests pledging support for the new Maryland effort and commenting on what they saw as its strengths and challenges. The American Farmland Trust representative called the concept a "critical model for the nation." Hortenstein suggested the biggest challenge would be the tradition of "local prerogative," but thought the approach of using incentives rather than regulations provided a chance to change that dynamic. "If counties have to compete," he said, "it may be a way to escape parochialism."[27]

Deford, the Maryland winemaker, concurred with "the need to commit public funds into land preservation efforts. It is the right time, if not a bit late," he said. "I can't see where there will be a great deal of resistance on this from any level." Houghton, a wealthy environmentalist from the Eastern Shore, agreed, saying it would help "preserve the way of life of the farmers and watermen."[28]

"I think it was pretty important," Griffin later said of the brunch, "because you had significant organizations represented with significant people and I thought that impressed Parris. They all were pretty much saying the same thing."[29]

Glendening indeed seemed gratified at the broad expression of support, but wanted to impress upon this group that he did not want them—or the members of their organizations—to cherry pick just the parts of the program they liked, principally the Rural Legacy effort. He wanted these environmental leaders to understand that along with protection of farms and open space, he also expected support for targeted growth.

"It is essential that we have a growing, vibrant economy without having sprawl," he said. "We're going to have a comprehensive program and I ask that you support all of the elements. We're going to say to local governments, you have to meet certain criteria, hard criteria, if you want any state participation. We're *not* going to take over local zoning. We're *not* saying you can't do it. But we'll say, 'If you want to do it, do it in the growth envelope.'

"As carrots, we will have a Small Communities Infrastructure Development Fund," the governor said, although he never made good on that pledge.[30]

Finally, he urged cooperation. "We need to come together aggressively for the full package," he said. "There will be substantial opposition, from the homebuilders, developers, and MACO. We need a massive education, awareness and public lobbying program by the beginning of the [legislative] session.

"If we don't turn this corner soon," he concluded, "I despair over what this state will look like."[31]

# Chapter 7

# Opposition Solidifies

Life on the State House second floor, where the governor and his top aides had their offices, suddenly became very busy. The leaves turned to their fall colors, the air turned crisp, and the staff turned its attention to the legislative session, only about sixty days away. The governor would be leaving town soon for an economic development trip to Korea and the Thanksgiving and Christmas holidays were fast approaching. Budget decisions had to be made by Christmas in order to get the thick, four-volume document to the printers in time to have it back for the opening of the General Assembly in early January. Decisions had to be made on a wide range of initiatives, legislation, staff assignments, appointments, and more. The Smart Growth workgroup no longer enjoyed the luxury of having the time to throw out ideas and debate possible strategies.

Kreitner convened the work group in early November to meet with the governor and figure out precisely how the Priority Funding Areas would work. The first order of business, however, was to decide, once and for all, the name of the overall proposal: it would be "Smart Growth and Neighborhood Conservation." Despite the governor's earlier misgivings, the group also agreed to call the land preservation program by its original name, "Rural Legacy."[1]

The group then moved into the details. Counties could designate areas as Priority Funding Areas only if they met a set of three state criteria: the areas had to be served by, or planned to be served by, sewer and water; the density of new residential development in the designated areas had to be at least five units per acre; and the overall PFA plan for any county had to be consistent with and sufficient to accommodate that county's projected growth.* State funding for growth would only be

---

*This was generally interpreted within the Office of Planning to mean capacity sufficient to accommodate twenty years of growth.

allowed in these locally approved growth areas. Exceptions would be permitted, but would have to be carefully defined in advance.

With regard to roads, the state would continue to support construction, but only if new roads were within or connected growth areas. Tax credits would be targeted to revitalization areas.

"There will be more financial support for Smart Growth Areas," the governor insisted. "With incentives and disincentives, we will drive the private market forces into Smart Growth areas."[2]

For the rest of the month, the outreach effort on Smart Growth was in full swing. Young met with county executives, officials from both the Maryland Municipal League and the Maryland Association of Counties and others. The idea was to line up supporters before the fight was actually joined. Someone in the group quoted Mark Twain saying, "When you need a friend, it is too late to make one."[3]

Already, however, opposition to whatever the governor intended to propose was solidifying. One new area of concern was the reaction of Maryland farmers to the new Rural Legacy Program. As part of the first-year, FY 98 funding of just under $11 million, the administration proposed using the proceeds from $3 million in state-backed General Obligation bonds plus $7.8 million from the real estate transfer tax that was otherwise earmarked for Program Open Space. The farm community saw in this a diversion of funds that might otherwise be used for farmland preservation.

Bill Knill, a farmer from Mt. Airy in Carroll County, was president of the Maryland Farm Bureau and very protective of the state's farmland preservation program. The Farm Bureau argued that any money for Rural Legacy should be funneled through the Maryland Agricultural Land Preservation Foundation, known as "MALPF," rather than through DNR. Their contention, DNR's Grant Dehart recalled, was that most of the land that would be protected under Rural Legacy was likely to be farmland, therefore the money should flow through—and be controlled by—MALPF.

"John Griffin strongly objected," Dehart later recounted. "He felt that would weaken the concept of Rural Legacy being for multiple resource protection."[4]

To counter this opposition, the governor and his staff decided to introduce as part of the Smart Growth package a "Right to Farm" bill[5] that would protect farmers from nuisance suits. These suits were often brought by city dwellers who had moved to the country, only to discover they did not like the wafting aroma of manure or the squeaks and rumble of farm tractors at dawn. The idea was that the Right to Farm bill would appease the farmers, who otherwise might oppose the funding mechanism for a major component of the Smart Growth initiative, the new Rural Legacy program. Once again, Glendening anticipated the opposition and lined up his defenses in advance.

The Right to Farm legislation would expand the definition of "agricultural operations" that are protected from certain private legal actions to include "any commercial activity conducted in conjunction with the cultivation, raising, harvesting, or production of a farm product, including the preparation for market, processing, transportation or sale of a farm product."

Once again the governor directed Young and other staff to talk up the program "with our friends," but cautioned sternly: "Put nothing in writing; talk conceptually."[6]

Despite the governor's warnings, Young reported back to the group, "I've gotten fairly specific: Rural Legacy, Smart Growth Areas (though I've told them we're still looking for input), brownfields (I said the governor is committed), tax incentives (we're looking toward incentives and disincentives, job creation, house renovation), and the Right to Farm bill (it needs to be strengthened)."

But Glendening's caginess troubled Jim Brady, who then was still the governor's economic development secretary. He said his associates in the business community were complaining to him that they were being kept in the dark. "We're creating problems—raising more problems than need be," he said.[7]

The need for a video illustrating the problem of sprawl and abandonment was again raised. Kreitner said he planned to write a "New Year's article" for one of the state's major newspapers that would "forecast what '97 will mean if we don't control growth." Nita Settina, a legislative aide to Griffin at DNR, said she would try to encourage influential *Baltimore Sun* environmental columnist Tom Horton to write an article about the importance of passing the new program.[8]

But Settina also warned that as important as the Smart Growth initiative might be to environmental groups, many were threatening to withhold their support in an effort to leverage Glendening into opposing projects they opposed, principally the Chapman's Landing development, a proposed highway bypass around Waldorf in Charles County, southeast of Washington, D.C., and the long controversial and hugely expensive Intercounty Connector (ICC), a proposed superhighway stretching from I-270 in Montgomery County eastward to I-95 in Prince George's County north of the Capital Beltway.

"They'll shoot down the growth package if you support the projects," she said without equivocation. "They'll say there is a lack of credibility by the governor. They have a grass roots opposition to these projects and a well-organized core. And, they say transportation as it relates to growth is not being addressed."[9]

This latter complaint about the program's failure to address transportation decision making persisted to the end of the Glendening years and beyond. Even Kreitner complained privately in those early days,

"There is no way to articulate what will be different regarding transportation than we have done before."[10]

Still, there were some reasons for optimism. Larsen reported that he had met with Tom Lewis and Joseph C. Bryce, the legislative assistants to the House Speaker and Senate president, respectively, and with Senator Frosh and that "a framework of agreement on brownfields" legislation had been reached.[11]

"From a press standpoint, brownfields was part of the package. But from a working standpoint, it was just a holdover from the prior session," Larsen recalled later. "It was delivered separately from a separate process. I guess brownfields was sort of our first foray into the revitalization stuff."[12]

In announcing to the staff the imminent agreement on brownfields, Larsen also said he had scheduled briefings for the Greater Baltimore Committee, a Baltimore-based social justice organization called BUILD, chambers of commerce, the Washington Board of Trade, homebuilders, and others.

The Baltimore-based 1000 Friends of Maryland group met with Glendening staff to offer public relations help. Baltimore planner Al Barry promised the group would try to be "the initiator of the public debate," and said the message would be, "We are not no-growth proponents. We are Smart Growth proponents."[13]

On December 5, Kreitner briefed the entire cabinet on the Smart Growth proposal, outlining a program designed to help more children walk to school, remove more nitrogen pollution from the bay, and improve the state's quality of life.

Seated at the center of a large U-shaped table in the ornate Reception Room just outside his second floor State House office, Glendening said: "The challenge is: there will be no immediate payoff. You have to have faith that in four or five years from now, we'll see significant change."[14]

## Legislative Reaction

The question now was: how would members of the legislature react? Glendening and his staff had managed to get through the fall without revealing too many details too early, but by mid-December, it was time for the administration to show its cards. The cabinet now knew most of the details, so it seemed inevitable that some of them would be leaked to the press. Better to tell lawmakers directly than have them read about the proposal in the newspapers.

Eight days before Christmas, Glendening and his staff briefed a group of General Assembly leaders about the Smart Growth initiative. Their reaction was generally supportive, yet scattered based on which parts of the initiative caught their eye. Some focused on where future school construction would occur; others on whether the state should try to limit construction on septic systems by favoring projects that are hooked into public sewers; still others on why the initiative failed to include provisions to address crime that was pushing residents out of places such as Baltimore.[15]

Most of the comments, however, were constructive attempts to make the initiative more palatable. That was a relief to staff who worried about outright opposition. There seemed to be recognition among the lawmakers that something was wrong with the state's development pattern and that something needed to be done. They seemed to agree there was a problem. The debate was over how to address it. For the members of Glendening's workgroup, that was good news. Debating policy was not only legitimate, it could be helpful. By contrast, if the legislators had just stridently opposed the plan, that would have meant bare-knuckle fighting. After the legislative battles over stadiums and gun control the previous year, no one had much of a stomach for that.

Many of the legislators' comments were strategic suggestions—both general and specific—on how best to get the legislation through the assembly. Delegate James Rosapepe of Prince George's County, for example, questioned the choice of the word *Rural* in the program title "Rural Legacy."

"The constituency for this is in the suburban areas," he said, acknowledging that the loss of farmland and open space seemed to be noticed most by those suburbanites whose homes, in many cases, were causing that loss. "You may not want to call it 'Rural.' It is more of a greenbelt concept. Call it the 'Greenbelt Legacy Program,' or the 'Green Legacy Program.'"[16]

Glendening said he was more concerned that the agricultural industry would not support the Rural Legacy Program because farmers would see it as a diversion of money that could have been used for farmland preservation. "Farmers won't support it, so we have to push this through over their objections," Glendening told the lawmakers.[17]

Delegate Barbara A Frush, a Democrat from Prince George's County, opined that the cause of sprawl in Baltimore City was "decay, crime and [failing] schools," issues not directly addressed in the draft legislation. Glendening acknowledged those problems, but said other smaller Maryland communities were suffering from downtown abandonment that seemed to have nothing to do with the problems afflicting Baltimore. "Crime had nothing to do with the decline in Cumberland or Easton," he said.[18]

Rosapepe jumped in again, saying he thought it was a mistake to exclude school construction funds from the list of funds that would be targeted only within Priority Funding Areas. Glendening had intentionally omitted reference to school construction funds in the legislation because he feared including a restriction on where those funds could be spent could rally rural lawmakers in opposition and sink the entire proposal.

Moreover, the governor knew he had the executive budgetary authority to direct where future school construction funds would be spent. Therefore, he thought it made no sense to encourage opposition unnecessarily. He knew the legislation would generate enough opposition as it was.

Senator Frosh, a thin, mustachioed lawyer who understood environmental issues probably better than anyone else in the legislature, immediately grasped the inside-outside strategy embodied in the separate Priority Funding Area and Rural Legacy legislation. "The strategy," he suggested, "should be to tie the two proposals together—to make one bill contingent on the passage of the others."[19] This concept was discussed by Glendening's legislative staff, but never acted upon. Although in both his public remarks and private lobbying Glendening always encouraged listeners to support the entire package rather than individual pieces of the legislation, the Smart Growth Areas and Rural Legacy bills were never formally linked to each other.

DNR's Griffin, knowing the potential power of the Rural Legacy argument, tried to sway the legislative leaders to the cause. "If we don't get in and save these remaining areas, they're gone," he said.[20]

Young, the Office of Planning deputy, agreed, offering up a statistic that, in different variations, was to become one of the governor's most frequently repeated sound bites: "If we don't do something, in the next twenty-five years we project five hundred thousand acres will be developed, which is larger than Baltimore County and Baltimore City combined, or larger than Montgomery and Howard counties combined, or larger than Prince George's and Howard counties. If past trends continue, we will consume as much land in central Maryland in the next twenty-five years as we have in the entire history of the state."[21]

Glendening appealed to the legislators' sense of right and wrong. "It is morally wrong," he said of the state's development pattern, "and expensive. We took fifty years to get there. We can't turn it around in one year. But we have to have a long-term view of what is best."[22]

# Chapter 8

# The General Assembly Battle

Two days after New Year's 1997, Governor Glendening drove to the *Baltimore Sun* offices on Calvert Street and rode the elevator up to the Editorial Department offices on the fifth floor. He was there to sell the idea of Smart Growth to the newspaper's editorial writers.

This was a pilgrimage the governor made prior to each legislative session. The tradition at the *Sun* was to hold meetings such as this exclusively with the newspaper's editorial board. Regular news reporters laboring away at their desks two floors below not only were not invited, they rarely knew such meetings were taking place or that the governor was even in their building unless they accidentally ran into him. It was done this way to keep intact the firewall that historically separated the news gatherers from the opinion makers. For the governor, it had the effect of allowing him to speak more freely than he would in front of news reporters jotting down his every word. It was an opportunity for him to make his case as persuasively as he could.

Welcomed by Editorial Page Editor Joseph R. L. Sterne, the governor briefed the small group of editorial writers about the various pieces of legislation he would back in the legislative session that was about to start. He reserved most of his time, however, to talk about the Smart Growth initiative. He encouraged the newspaper to invest time on the issue, saying the *Sun* could be "helpful in framing the debate," and indicated that the newspaper's home city would benefit from a program that emphasized redevelopment and discouraged suburban migration. He talked about the Rural Legacy program as fostering a "European-style" development pattern with greenbelts around rural hamlets.[1]

The reaction by the writers was surprisingly skeptical—skeptical anything would pass and skeptical that it would have any effect even if it did. Besides, asked one of the writers, what's wrong with wanting to live in the suburbs?[2]

Finally, at a meeting in College Park of the state's volunteer, DNR-sponsored "Tributary Teams" on January 11, Governor Glendening finally made public the details of his Smart Growth initiative. Speaking to a sympathetic audience of volunteers appointed to restore the bay's rivers and streams, Glendening said, "Protection of the bay starts on the land—not on the water." He called sprawl "a disease that is eating away at America."[3]

Immediate reaction to the new initiative was mixed. Senate President Thomas V. Mike Miller Jr., a Democrat from Prince George's County who was often more interested in the politics of legislation than the substance, warned that farmers were already worried that growth restrictions could adversely affect their land values. The Bay Foundation's Will Baker, on the other hand, suggested that the proposal did not go far enough, although he said CBF would make a vote on the Smart Growth measure "a referendum on the Bay."

Over the next couple weeks, the five pieces of legislation that made up the Smart Growth initiative were introduced:

- "Smart Growth" and Neighborhood Conservation—"Smart Growth" Areas;[4]
- "Smart Growth" and Neighborhood Conservation—Rural Legacy Program;[5]
- Brownfields—Voluntary Cleanup and Revitalization Programs;[6]
- Job Creation Tax Credit Act of 1997;[7]
- Maryland Right to Farm.[8]

In addition, a sixth component was introduced as a budget program: a $300,000 pilot program called Live Near Your Work through which the state, local governments, and participating employers would provide stipends of $1,000 each, $3,000 total, to home buyers who purchased homes in certain designated revitalization areas.

The first success was with the brownfields legislation, which had been nearly two years in the making. The 1997 version was introduced as an emergency bill, not because there was any brownfields "emergency," but because the compromise on the legislation that Larsen had struck between the environmentalists and the business community was so tenuous that advocates wanted to make sure that as soon as the bill passed both houses of the legislature, it could be put on the governor's desk for his immediate signature before anyone changed their mind.

On February 17, only one month into the three-month session, the Senate approved the bill on a 46–0 vote. Seven days later the House agreed, 137–0. The unanimous votes obviously provided the supermajority required by the rules for passage of emergency legislation. The measure was immediately signed into law by Glendening.[9]

But the Smart Growth Areas, Rural Legacy, and Right to Farm bills all faced stiff resistance from different factions and for different reasons.

Lobbyists for Maryland counties attacked the Smart Growth Areas legislation in three specific areas, although their opposition to increased state involvement in local land use issues in general was their fundamental concern. There was no amendment that could fix that problem.

The counties specifically opposed the bill's proposed requirement that new residential density within proposed Priority Funding Areas be a minimum of five units per acre, a density they felt was much too high. To local land use officials, "density" was a dirty word and they did not want to be forced to push more of it on constituents who clearly saw no advantage to living next to more intensive development.

The counties also objected to giving the Maryland Office of Planning veto authority over local PFA plans. Again, they did not want the state telling them what to do.

Finally, they felt the legislation simply failed to address the needs of rural crossroads, or villages, which dot the countryside in Maryland's more rural counties. Ignoring those tiny villages, they said, meant that those areas could never receive state financial assistance for road improvements or other infrastructure needs that larger Priority Funding Areas would be eligible to receive. It was unfair to the citizens who lived in those crossroads communities, they said.

Opposition to the proposed Rural Legacy program came mostly from farmers who saw the new land protection program as a drain on already scarce funds for farmland preservation. Glendening and his staff also had to convince Rural Legacy supporters to resist the temptation to support the Rural Legacy bill while abandoning other components of the Smart Growth package. Publicly and privately, Glendening tried to get supporters of one part of the package to support all parts. They were linked, he argued, and must be passed together.

## Right to Farm

The Right to Farm legislation was almost an afterthought in the compilation of Smart Growth ideas. It was added to the mix primarily to appease farmers, who otherwise saw nothing in the Smart Growth initiative for them except the loss of farm protection funds to Rural Legacy. It was designed to protect farmers from "nuisance suits" filed by residents transplanted from urban or suburban localities who discovered they did not like the sounds or odor of agricultural practices.[10]

"Cows stink. Every Marylander should know that basic fact about farming," began one *Baltimore Sun* story[11] about a hearing on the legislation. Upperco farmer Wayne Armacost, whose family had been farming in Baltimore County for seven generations, testified that complaints by neighbors and the resulting repeated visits by local and state inspectors bordered on harassment. Dust from plowing or odors from manure, hogs, cows, or chickens is just part of farming, he told lawmakers.

But some of Armacost's neighbors said the problem was much worse than typical farm smells, comparing the odor more to a septic system than a stable.

In the end, the Right to Farm legislation became something of an asterisk to the Smart Growth initiative, the only component of the legislative package to be defeated. Not many Smart Growth proponents remember it was even proposed. The bill fell victim to opposition from, of all quarters, environmentalists, who read into its provisions the possibility of opening Maryland to the kind of large-scale hog farming operations that had caused serious environmental damage in North Carolina and other states.

Thomas Grasso, then the Maryland director for the Chesapeake Bay Foundation, argued that all farmers do not deserve the same protection and that those with large livestock herds—or which have to obtain pollution permits from the state Department of Environment—should be exempted.

The measure passed in the Senate, but became bottled up in the House Environmental Matters Committee despite support from the committee chairman, Delegate Ron Guns, who said he sympathized with the farmers. Quietly, the environmentalists lined up the votes in the House committee to kill the legislation and the fight was over almost before the Glendening team realized the bill was even in trouble.

Ironically, the Right to Farm bill never enjoyed much support from the farmers it was intended to help, who—led by Maryland Farm Bureau lobbyist Jack Miller—were hostile to the whole notion of "Smart Growth."

"Our policy was to have this umbrella group" representing a broad array of interests, including farmers, Kreitner later recalled. "We were saying, 'We're going to do all these things [in the Smart Growth Areas and Rural Legacy legislation] that may impact farmers in one way, but in another way we're going to give them something for being part of it all."[12]

"It was really loading up the Christmas tree to try to get as many things as possible for as many groups as possible," Larsen said of the decision to include the Right to Farm bill as part of the Smart Growth package.[13]

"It was something they claimed they needed," Kreitner said. "But the farmers didn't join in to help with Smart Growth, so we didn't get any buy-in for it." As a result, the administration did not expend much political capital to save the legislation when it got in trouble.[14]

As he thought through the strategy needed to pass the Smart Growth program, Kreitner said he vividly recalled the nasty attacks the farming interests, homebuilders, and local governments had made on the Barnes Commission recommendations seven years earlier and said he had never quite gotten over it. ("The Farm Bureau, in particular, had characterized the efforts to limit sprawl as un-American and communism," Kreitner bitterly recalled.) In the intervening years, he spent a lot of time trying to get the farming interests on board, but without much success. At the first Senate committee hearing on the Smart Growth Areas law in 1997, the normally mild-mannered planning director decided to make a point to the farmers about the breadth of support the Smart Growth concept enjoyed.[15]

After he and Larsen testified before the committee, Kreitner returned to a front row seat in the audience next to Miller, who had registered to testify that the Farm Bureau opposed the legislation. The next panel of witnesses to support the bill, arranged in advance by Kreitner, included four clergy from different denominations—Jewish, Catholic, Protestant.

Miller, Kreitner recalled years later, leaned over to him and asked testily, "Who are you going to call next, Jesus Christ?" To which Kreitner said he replied, "If we need him [to line up votes] in the House, Jack, we will."[16]

## Rural Legacy

The most popular bill in the Smart Growth package was the Rural Legacy legislation. After all, it was hard for lawmakers to oppose the idea of buying up the development rights on farms and some of the state's most beautiful natural areas. With many citizens looking for ways to stop development in their areas, it was an idea that quickly sparked fairly broad support.

Only the farmers seemed opposed. But their opposition was overcome the way so many other legislative problems are resolved in Annapolis: with money. The Farm Bureau, led by Carroll County farmer Bill Knill, had put out a flier opposing Rural Legacy. When DNR's Griffin saw it, recalled staff aide Grant Dehart, he was livid.[17] Farm Bureau lobbyist Jack Miller stepped in to broker a compromise.

At the time, the farmland preservation program was getting about 14.2 percent of the annual revenue from the real estate transfer tax. Miller cut a deal that increased that share to 17 percent in exchange for the Farm Bureau's support for selling bonds to finance Rural Legacy acquisitions. After that, opposition to the bill for the most part disappeared.[18]

## "The Goldilocks Approach"

The counties and other interest groups, however, recognized that the meat of the Smart Growth initiative was not the Rural Legacy bill, but rather the Smart Growth Areas Act. If they were not careful, that was where the state might secure a foothold in the local planning decision process.

Leading the attack for the counties was David Bliden, a lawyer who was executive director of the Maryland Association of Counties, and Kris Hughes, a planner who represented MACO in most of the work sessions and internal meetings on the bill.

"There was a lot of time spent with the Blidens and Hugheses of the world," Larsen remembered. "My sense was that they wanted to kill the thing from day one. But they did what they had to do when the governor has a bill: you meet with people and talk. But I always felt like we were the ones making concessions. The governor, of course, had been a county executive and he wanted them on board. But my perception was that for all the time we put into [meeting with them], they weren't really buying into anything."[19]

Before even a month of the ninety-day session had elapsed, MACO had honed in on the heart of the Smart Growth Areas legislation: the provision stipulating a proposed density in Priority Funding Areas of five units per acre.

"It was a number that was really based on a fair amount of analysis of existing development patterns—not just how we were going to deal with development outside of developed areas," said Kreitner, whose Office of Planning came up with the recommended density level. "We had felt that [five units per acre] would actually make a difference—a considerable difference—and it would also address some of the underdevelopment within areas already served by water and sewer as well."[20]

"What it came down to was a lot of debate about Columbia," the "new town" built beginning in 1960s by famed developer James Rouse in Howard County, halfway between Baltimore and Washington. MACO, Kreitner said, sounded an alarm. Five units per acre, the county lobbyists said, "would force something denser than Columbia."[21]

But Kreitner said, "Most of the world involved in Smart Growth felt that Columbia wasn't dense enough to begin with and that there were problems as a result of it, and that if you continued to develop at that scale, the impact wasn't going to be that significant."[22]

MACO, of course, disagreed. Kris Hughes and Joseph Rutter, then the planning director for Howard County, led the charge. In a meeting with administration officials, Rutter argued that five units per acre was simply too restrictive. By contrast, he said two units per acre—that is to say, minimum half-acre lots in areas that were supposed to be designated for growth—was too relaxed a standard. Columbia, he said, had an average density of 3.67 units per acre. Therefore, he suggested, an average minimum density of about 3.5 units per acre was just about right. He called it the "Goldilocks" approach—not too big, not too small, but just right.[23]

Despite opposition from the administration, the county lobbyists had their way and the legislation was amended to reduce the minimum density in PFAs from five units an acre to 3.5

Related to that was a provision in the original legislation that would require county governments to develop their Priority Funding Area plans and submit them to the state's Office of Planning to determine if they were consistent with the requirements and goals of the legislation. Implicit was the perception that Office of Planning approval of local PFA plans would be required. That clearly represented more authority than the counties wanted the state to have. Again, the county lobbyists worked to whittle back the state's authority. By the time they were through, the legislation allowed the Office of Planning to "comment" on PFA plans, but denied the state veto authority.

After the Smart Growth Areas Act became law, the Office of Planning devised a clever way around this restriction. First, they required that PFAs be specified on maps. As state planners reviewed and "commented" upon each county-drawn PFA map, areas that were considered inconsistent with the Smart Growth law (e.g., areas not served or planned to be served by sewer and water or, more likely, areas that would provide development capacity well beyond the amount needed to satisfy the county's projected growth over the next twenty years) were highlighted with hatch marks in a way that separated them from the rest of a county's PFA.

From each county's perspective, the "comment areas" were still part of their officially designated PFA. But the state treated the "comment areas" as if they were outside the PFA. Maps showing the comment areas were circulated to all agencies with programs covered by the PFA law and the governor directed the agencies to refuse to fund projects in those areas. This approach had almost the same effect as if the state had veto authority over county PFA plans.[24]

## Rural Villages

The dispute over the exclusion of rural crossroads or villages from the legislation was somewhat different. The team representing the governor acknowledged the omission was an oversight and worked with the counties to draft mutually acceptable language to assure those hamlets were not forever denied state assistance for growth. At the same time, however, the administration team worried about inadvertently turning these villages into large-scale growth areas.

"We spent days with Bliden and Hughes going back and forth with this," remembered Kreitner.[25]

The final compromise added language to the legislation creating a special category of PFAs called "Rural Villages" that differentiated them from incorporated municipalities and defined them as follows:

> "Rural Village" means a rural village, village center, or other unincorporated area that is primarily residential, including an area with historic qualities, that is located in an otherwise rural or agricultural area and for which new growth, if any, would derive primarily from in-fill development or limited peripheral expansion.[26]

Also added to the legislation was a definition for "limited peripheral expansion": "Development that is contiguous to an existing community and does not increase the size of the existing community or village by more than 10% of the existing number of dwelling units."[27] As opposed to the bitterness generated by debate over minimum densities for PFAs or other provisions in the bill, there was general agreement by all parties that the inclusion of the "Rural Villages" section improved the legislation.

## Calling the House's Bluff

As the session drew toward a close in early April 1997, it appeared the Smart Growth package was headed to approval. Most of the contentious issues had been compromised, the environmentalists were on board, mayors and other urban supporters were behind it, the builders and the business community had adopted a more or less neutral position, and the counties felt they had at least addressed what they saw as the legislation's most onerous provisions. The only thing that stood between Glendening and passage of the legislation was the same conservative House committee chairman and another dose of gubernatorial politics.

The Smart Growth Areas bill, the lynchpin of the package, rested in the House Environmental Matters Committee, chaired by Cecil County Delegate Ron Guns. And there it sat, bottled up by a chairman who felt the state was reaching too far into the business of local government. Moreover, his boss, House Speaker Cas Taylor, a rural conservative in his own right, was still toying with the idea of challenging the politically weakened Glendening in the following year's gubernatorial primary. He had little incentive to make Glendening look good. Passing the centerpiece of Glendening's 1997 legislative agenda would make the governor look strong; defeating it would reinforce the perception that Glendening was politically weak and vulnerable. Moreover, Taylor and Guns knew that if the House passed the legislation, there was little doubt the Senate would follow suit.

MACO, recalled Kreitner, "did not have the votes [to kill the legislation]. They definitely didn't have it on the Senate side. They thought they had it on the House side with Guns. It was clear that every time we met with Guns, he had stuff from [MACO's] Kris Hughes. We'd go in and [the lobbyists for the counties] would be piling out of his office."[28]

Larsen, the governor's chief legislative lobbyist, agreed: "I think Guns was their ace in the hole. They perceived Ron as their man to stop it. Whenever we had a meeting, it was preceded by a MACO meeting. It was like Ron [Guns] was getting his negotiating instructions from them."[29]

The standoff festered for several days as Larsen and other administration lobbyists tried in vain to convince Guns to bring the bill up for a vote. Glendening met with Speaker Taylor and President Miller and told the two presiding officers as forcefully as he could that he wanted his Smart Growth legislation enacted. Yet, the stalemate continued.

Any legislation not enacted by midnight on the session's final night was dead. With the session's final day fast approaching, Glendening decided to call the legislators' bluff. Here's how he did it:

At the end of almost every legislative session, the governor of Maryland introduces a supplement to his original budget, appropriating revenue that might have come to the state since the original budget was introduced, or reappropriating funds that were earmarked for programs in the original budget but had already been cut from the spending plan by the General Assembly. Compared with other states, the governor of Maryland has extraordinary budgetary power—more authority than just about any of his forty-nine counterparts. The governor prepares the budget and legislators cannot increase it or transfer funds from one budgeted item to another. They can only cut. As a result, they are heavily dependent on the goodwill of the governor to fund their pet projects and priority programs. Conversely, the governor usually makes sure to withhold funds for those projects until the end of the session to leverage them to the maximum.

The end-of-session supplemental budget, therefore, often becomes the grease with which other, unrelated legislative deals are lubricated. It is the final opportunity in each legislative session for lawmakers to make good on campaign promises, build their resumes or bring projects home to their districts and constituents. And in exchange, the governor usually manages to find the votes he needs to pass his priority legislation, which always seems to be mysteriously stuck in committee until he does so.

When the House Environmental Matters Committee refused the entreaties of the governor's staff to vote on the Smart Growth Areas bill, however, Governor Glendening let legislative leaders know that there would be no supplemental budget introduced until that legislation reached the House floor.

In retaliation, House leaders refused to act on an unrelated school funding measure that Glendening wanted passed until the governor released the supplemental spending plan.

"I'm making it clear that I'm holding the supplemental budget until I get a good, strong [Smart Growth] bill," Glendening told the *Washington Post*.[30]

The press speculated the issue had been caught between the competing gubernatorial ambitions of Glendening and Taylor. "I keep hearing that and I'm appalled at what appears to be going on. I don't understand the motivation," said Glendening, who undoubtedly understood the motivation as well as anyone in Annapolis. "I think it would be a tragedy if politics reared its ugly head on an issue so important,"[31] he said with a straight face.

Taylor, of course, denied politics had anything to do with it. The legislation was complicated and interest groups, including rural counties, had raised important concerns, the speaker said.

For more than a week, the two sides waited—Glendening waiting for the legislation to move to the floor, and legislative leaders waiting for pressure to mount on Glendening to produce the supplemental budget.

"It made Annapolis a pressure cooker like I'd never seen before," recalled Kreitner.[32]

Lawmakers saw their pet projects going down the drain and they beat on the Speaker and the Senate President to convince the governor to relent and introduce the supplemental budget. The governor, said Larsen, "was excoriated by the presiding officers daily, and by the rank-and-file."[33]

Suddenly, unexpectedly, in the final week of the session, Kreitner received a phone call from Taylor inviting him to join Guns and him at a private dinner in the Speaker's suite at the Lowe's Annapolis Hotel, about three blocks from the State House.

"This was at the point where nothing was moving. The governor had made it clear he wanted a bill and that no supplemental was going to be submitted until he had a bill. Cas was really feeling the pressure. Cas was trying to understand it. He clearly wanted to find a way to get Guns to move."[34]

The dinner meeting went late into the night. "We killed some wine that night," Kreitner recalled.[35] The discussion ended with an agreement for a meeting between Guns and his Senate counterpart, Brian Frosh, the next day. But when the next day arrived, the two refused to meet.

Larsen convinced Frosh to go to lunch with him at Harry Browne's, a restaurant across the street from the State House. They were joined by Senator Michael Collins, a Democrat from Baltimore County. "Collins was trying to help out. Collins liked the governor and the governor was good to Collins, so Collins was trying to be an emissary with Brian, trying to get Brian to engage more," Larsen said.[36] But by the end of lunch, it appeared nothing could revive the negotiations.

"I was desperate at that point," Larsen said. "It was my first year as a [chief] legislative officer, this was the governor's signature bill, and I remember leaving lunch as dejected as I had ever been, not only in the process, but in my career as a legislative aide. It just wasn't going to happen."[37]

Larsen returned to his office on the State House's second floor. "I was actually getting ready to go in and tell the governor that we had not reached agreement when I got a phone call that in the intervening time they had gotten together." Apparently, Collins took Frosh for a walk and they had ended up in Guns's office, where they broke the deadlock. "As of lunchtime, it was done, dead, and I was sitting in my office trying to figure out, 'How do I break the news of this failure to the governor?' And, lo and behold, I get this phone call."[38]

**Fig. 8.1.** Chief Legislative Officer Steven B. Larsen had the difficult task of shepherding Glendening's Smart Growth package through the General Assembly, often over the opposition of county officials. Photo courtesy of the *Baltimore Sun*.

The House leaders had blinked, the Environmental Matters Committee would pass the legislation, and the governor could introduce his supplemental budget.

The legislation still faced other hurdles. Its passage appeared in jeopardy again when Montgomery and Prince George's County officials realized they were not going to receive nearly as much new school funding in the supplemental budget as was budgeted for Baltimore City schools. Later, the legislation was almost derailed again by rural concerns over whether already approved highway projects would be stopped by the Smart Growth law—a problem remedied by a craftily worded advisory letter from Assistant Attorney General Robert Zarnoch, the chief counsel to the General Assembly. But it was Collins's quiet diplomacy, fueled by Glendening's threat to withhold the supplemental budget, that finally broke the logjam.

"That was absolutely the catalyst, the *sine qua non*, for making this happen. This would not have happened had the governor not done this," Larsen said. "Cas Taylor would not have engaged himself and his staff to motivate Ron [Guns] in any way, shape or form but for the [threat to withhold] the supplemental. Cas came from a rural, western Maryland area. He was not inclined to do anything like this nor to give the governor any political credit."[39]

The governor's budget threat, Kreitner said, "was the sort of thing that could never be done twice in that way. It was a one-time thing because the legislature was caught off-guard by it. They couldn't come up with any way to deal with it.[40]

"The other thing it meant to me is that it was a very, very powerful motivating source, because it said, 'This guy is going to put everything on the line for this.' It made you think, 'We've got to run with this. We've got to make this successful.' It was one of those things where you can't fail."[41]

Larsen agreed. "You realized you needed to deliver a bill. We realized we didn't want to compromise too much so that we ended up with a complete 'nothing-burger,'" he said, employing the same pejorative description often used by detractors to describe the 1992 Growth Act. "We didn't want to betray the courageous nature of the governor's act by coming up with a weak bill. And that just added to the whole pressure cooker environment at the end."[42]

Once on the floor of the House and Senate, the entire Smart Growth package drew strong support. Earlier in the session, the brownfields legislation had passed unanimously in both houses. The Job Creation Tax Credit legislation,[43] which simply modified an existing Job Creation Tax Credit program by setting up a lower qualifying threshold for jobs created within Priority Funding Areas, was approved unanimously in the Senate in mid-March and by a 137–1 vote in the House on April 7. An identical House version was also approved the same day.

Once the Environmental Matters Committee released the Smart Growth Areas Act, both it and the companion Rural Legacy legislation were approved by the full House on the same day, April 3, the Thursday before the following Monday's midnight adjournment. Rural Legacy was approved, 131–8, and the Smart Growth Areas Act was passed, 126–15. Four days later, on the session's final day, both measures were approved by the Senate, 44–0 for Rural Legacy[44] and 41–5 for the Smart Growth Areas Act.[45]

Without ever being mentioned by name, the Live Near Your Work pilot program was approved as part of the General Assembly's approval of the overall state budget for Fiscal Year 1998. With the exception of the Right to Farm bill, Glendening's entire Smart Growth and Neighborhood Conservation initiative had been enacted.

"The governor thinks of all the measures before the legislature this year, Smart Growth will have perhaps the greatest impact on how families and communities live," said Glendening's press secretary, Judi Scioli.[46]

Senator Frosh said, "It means we won't be throwing state money after the last townhouse out in some cornfield somewhere."[47]

Editorially, the *Post* seemed to agree: "This legislation doesn't guarantee the preservation of pristine territory in Maryland in the future, but it does apply the brakes to disorderly growth that costs the state dearly. That is a considerable improvement, with a payoff that could be good for generations."[48]

For the first time, the state had decided to use location as a primary criterion for deciding where it should invest taxpayer funds. For the first time, the state had the semblance of a statewide land use plan, although no one was so politically insensitive as to call it that in public. Yet, taken together, the Smart Growth Areas Act and the Rural Legacy program would result in a locally drawn, statewide plan in which local governments would designate the precise areas where they wanted the state to invest in growth as well as the precise areas where they wanted the state to invest in land preservation. Smart Growth was never sold as a "statewide plan," but that was the net effect.

Less than two weeks later, after the legislature had adjourned and left town, Governor Parris N. Glendening publicly reviewed his legislative accomplishments at an event on Lower Eastern Shore and began ratcheting up the rhetoric surrounding his brand new Smart Growth initiative.

"One of our biggest accomplishments was for the environment," he told a small crowd gathered at the Salisbury Zoo. "We enacted Smart Growth, one of the nation's strongest growth management policies."[49]

# Chapter 9

## Momentum, Implementation,
## and Resistance

In 1998, Parris Glendening was blessed by drawing Ellen R. Sauerbrey as his election opponent for a second time. In their first meeting, it had been an open seat and both candidates were relatively unknown to the public, especially Sauerbrey. In this rematch, Glendening had the clear advantage of incumbency, plenty of time to prepare and an opportunity to define Sauerbrey in his own terms. Glendening would later interpret his strong victory in this election as a mandate for stronger protection of the environment and support for his fledgling Smart Growth initiative.

Four years earlier, Sauerbrey had upset veteran Congresswoman Helen Delich Bentley in the GOP primary (52 percent to 38 percent in a three-way race) and almost scored an even more stunning upset in the November general election. In a state in which registered Democrats outnumbered Republicans by two-to-one, Sauerbrey came within 5,993 votes of beating Glendening out of more than 1.4 million votes cast. The election was only settled after absentee ballots were tallied and Sauerbrey unsuccessfully challenged the results in court. It may have been the closest gubernatorial election in Maryland history; it certainly was one of the bitterest.

On a personal level, neither Sauerbrey nor Glendening could conceal their visceral dislike for each other. In one incident, they shouted at each other while appearing together live on a prime time national TV talk show.

The two candidates were political opposites, he the confident and calculating Democratic liberal; she the upstart, revolution-minded Republican conservative. Glendening had the backing of the state's urbanized core, its black and other minority citizens, teachers and other union members, and environmentalists. In 1994, Glendening had carried only three of the state's twenty-four major jurisdictions, Baltimore City and the two suburban Washington counties, Montgomery and Prince George's, but there were enough votes there for him to barely win.

Sauerbrey had the backing of the rural areas outside the densely populated Baltimore-Washington corridor, the business community, and Republicans and independents eager to break the Democratic Party's long dominance in Annapolis. In a portent of how politics would play out in Maryland in the years to come, the two campaigns struggled over who would control the suburban vote—precisely where many of the formerly urban residents had fled.

Their policy differences played out on virtually every issue, but on none as starkly as on the environment. As a state delegate from Baltimore County and minority leader in the House of Delegates, Sauerbrey had compiled a record on environmental issues that the nonprofit Maryland League of Conservation Voters rated as dead last among the state's 188 legislators. No one, the league said, was worse on environmental issues.

Glendening, meanwhile, had pushed through an array of Chesapeake Bay protection measures and, most notably, had championed passage of the Smart Growth initiative just the year before. As a result, he had become the darling of the state's environmental movement. Glendening may not have done everything the environmental community asked of him, but he had done enough to credibly run for reelection in 1998 as "the environmental candidate." That was what he had every intention of doing.

Glendening's environmental record was good, but stacked up against Sauerbrey's, it looked even better than it was. To those who cared about environmental issues, simply the thought of Sauerbrey becoming Governor sent shudders through the ranks. There was a running joke among environmentalists about how the Chesapeake Bay Foundation should prohibit its members from displaying its famous "Save the Bay" bumper sticker on any bumper that also displayed a Sauerbrey sticker.

From the time the Smart Growth legislation was enacted in April 1997 through to the November 1998 election, Glendening and his staff rolled out one environmental or Smart Growth event after another. Glendening never expected the environmental community to match the ability of business interests to raise campaign funds (and, in the end, Sauerbrey raised more money overall than Glendening), but the governor and his campaign aides knew the environmentalists could energize a large network of zealous activists needed to staff phone banks, pass out literature, or otherwise toil in the reelection effort.

"He's always pretty much balanced the environmental and economic development interests, [but] now he's tilting more green," observed State Senator Thomas McLain Middleton, a Democrat and farmer from Charles County. Developers are reliable sources of campaign donations, he said, but "developers don't get you the votes."[1]

As the Smart Growth legislation was about to go into effect in June 1997, Glendening transferred John W. Frece, then communications director and head of his press office, to the newly created position of Special

Assistant for Smart Growth. Frece was to be responsible for responding to media inquiries about the initiative, coordinating the activities of state agencies in support of Smart Growth, and crafting the message used to explain the initiative to the public, elected officials, and the press. He was to be a single point of contact for all Smart Growth inquiries. Frece also began writing speeches for the governor for Smart Growth issues or events.

"All I want you to do," Glendening told Frece as they stood by the fireplace in the governor's State House office and discussed the new assignment, "is change the culture."[2]

The following week, eight hundred people showed up for a Smart Growth conference in Baltimore that had expected to attract five hundred. "This is indicative of the enthusiasm surrounding this topic," Glendening gushed. "President Clinton and Vice President Gore are also enthusiastic. I saw Vice President Gore twice in the last two weeks. We discussed Smart Growth. He has been telling everyone, 'Look at Maryland's example.'"[3]

Indeed, outside recognition for the Maryland program began to pour in. Almost before the ink was dry on the Maryland legislation, nationally syndicated columnist Neal R. Peirce penned an article that began: "The other 49 states should take an early, hard look at Maryland's breakthrough 'Smart Growth' policy. . . . Finally, one American state has done a reality check, recognized sprawl development's incredibly heavy costs, and started thinking about potential savings—fiscal, social, environmental—from curbing state subsidies."[4]

An opinion column in the *Cleveland Plain Dealer* in June was addressed directly to that year's crop of Ohio gubernatorial candidates: "To Bob Taft, Lee Fisher and the others who dream of being Ohio's next governor, I have two words of advice: 'smart growth'. . . . I believe the candidate who gets out front first promoting the concept of smart growth will be a winner."[5]

In July, twenty states sent representatives to a Smart Growth conference in Baltimore put together by Glendening's staff in cooperation with the National Governors' Association. Articles appeared in St. Louis, New York, and elsewhere about the Maryland experiment and as the election drew closer, momentum behind the Smart Growth effort began to build.

## The ICC

One problem that threatened to explode before the election, however, was a forty-year-old dispute over whether to build a major highway across Montgomery County, the populous suburb of Washington, D.C. Long on county master plans, the road would be built north of and parallel to the Capital Beltway, connecting the I-270 corridor that runs northwest from Washington toward Frederick with the I-95 corridor that runs northeast through the center of the state. As a county executive and in his early

**Fig. 9.1.** Glendening became increasingly worried about the environmental impact of building the Intercounty Connector (ICC) and, instead, proposed to improve existing roads and intersections in the corridor. Photo courtesy of the *Baltimore Sun.*

years as governor, Glendening was a strong proponent of building the Intercounty Connector, better known as the ICC. The road was strongly supported by the business community, especially the powerful Washington Board of Trade, was editorially supported by the influential *Washington Post*, and was consistent with Glendening's goal of becoming the "economic development governor." Many business leaders financially supported Glendening's candidacy for governor because of his unwavering support for the ICC.

But environmentalists vehemently opposed the highway, saying it would seriously damage a series of stream valleys the road would cross. Moreover, they disputed the central claim of proponents that the road would relieve congestion on the Capital Beltway, citing government studies that showed the ICC would have very little impact on Beltway traffic. This, of course, was a difficult argument to make to a public that believed the only answer to gridlock was to build bigger and wider roads. Finally, they argued that the huge expense of the highway would mean less money was available for transit improvements or other needed transportation projects elsewhere.

Glendening, edging closer to the environmentalists' point of view, found himself caught in a political squeeze in an election year. He responded by trotting out a tried-and-true government solution: another study. He appointed a group of national transportation experts to a new panel called the Transportation Solutions Group* and asked them to review the transportation needs of the entire suburban Washington region, including transit, highway improvement projects, and the ICC. Although the group was widely criticized as being stacked with pro-highway consultants, Glendening gave the study group until mid-1999 to report their findings—well after the 1998 election would be over.

## Pfiesteria

In the run-up to the '98 election, even environmental disasters seemed to turn in Glendening's favor. After an outbreak of the fish-killing microbe Pfiesteria piscicida in rivers on the Lower Eastern Shore in the summer of 1997, Glendening closed three rivers and gained national headlines as the first prominent elected official to link the microbe to human illnesses. In a very public search for solutions, he hosted a multistate conference that

---

*The Transportation Solutions Group was chaired by Thomas B. Deen, an engineer and consultant and former executive director of the Transportation Research Board at the U.S. National Academy of Sciences and the National Academy of Engineering. Members are listed in the Report of the Transportation Solutions Group, July 15, 1999.

received favorable press coverage. Concluding that the outbreak was caused by the excessive poultry waste Eastern Shore farmers spread on their fields as fertilizer, Glendening introduced legislation in 1998 that called for an unprecedented and mandatory restriction on how much fertilizer farmers may apply to their fields. Environmentalists were wowed, but chicken producers were enraged.

The poultry industry has become hugely important to the economy on the "Delmarva Peninsula." But when the head of one of Maryland's major chicken producers threatened to pull his company out of Maryland in retaliation, Glendening said, "If someone were pouring a carcinogenic chemical into a stream in your neighborhood and the company said, 'Don't make us quit doing this or we'll leave,' no one would say, 'Okay, go ahead and pour it.'"[6]

In just a few short months, Glendening had sided with the environmentalists against big business, highway builders, farmers, and the state's agribusiness.

## Rural Legacy

Throughout the summer of 1997, staff at the Department of Natural Resources worked behind the scenes to set the new Rural Legacy program in motion. They developed a guidebook for how the program would work, circulated it to local governments, land trusts, and other interested organizations for feedback, and held a series of regional meetings to discuss the kinds of lands the state wanted to preserve and how the application process would work. They set January 31, 1998, as the first deadline for interested groups to submit applications to have specific geographic areas designated as Rural Legacy areas. Privately, however, staff worried the number of initial applicants might be embarrassingly small, so there was considerable relief when twenty-three submissions from all over the state were submitted by the deadline.

The Rural Legacy program was designed to be a departure from past land preservation practices, which had often been criticized as ineffective because of their piecemeal, farm-by-farm, or parcel-by-parcel approach. Often farms or properties were protected without any relationship to any other protected properties or any broader strategy to protect the surrounding area. The criterion for saving a particular farm often seemed to be nothing more than that the farmer had applied and his number had been called.

The goal of Rural Legacy, by contrast, was to identify large, contiguous tracts of land that were still undeveloped or at least were not overly fragmented by development. To be eligible for Rural Legacy funds, such lands had to feature multiple resources, such as scenic or historic value, prime agricultural soils, wetlands, buffers along waterways, old growth forests, wildlife habitat, buffers around drinking water reservoirs, or areas that would serve as greenbelts to protect the character of small towns or other communities. The more of these traits an area exhibited, the more likely it was that sponsors would receive state funding.

While the legislation authorized purchases of land in fee simple, the governor and his Smart Growth advisers anticipated that Rural Legacy funds would be used primarily to purchase development rights on targeted properties, leaving ownership and usage in the hands of existing landowners and keeping the property on local tax rolls. The state had no interest in owning farms or other lands around the state, but this approach generally made it impossible to provide public access to lands being protected with taxpayer dollars.

The other new and critically important criterion that had to be met before an area could be declared eligible for Rural Legacy funds was an estimate of "the degree of threat to the resources and character of the area . . . as reflected by patterns and trends of development and landscape modifications in and surrounding the proposed Rural Legacy Area."[7] This drew an unmistakable linkage between the effects of sprawl development and the state's loss of farmland, forests, and other scenic or ecologically significant areas. The state had never before made such an explicit connection.

For the next five months, the newly appointed, eleven-member Rural Legacy Advisory Committee[8] reviewed the applications, divided into teams to make site visits, listened to presentations by land trusts or other proposal sponsors, and ranked each of the applications. The rankings, in turn, were reviewed by a Rural Legacy Board made up of the secretaries of Natural Resources and Agriculture and the director of the Office of Planning, and were ultimately submitted to the governor for his approval.

To Glendening, of course, this was much more than just an exercise in land preservation. For him, the first award of Rural Legacy grants represented an opportunity to stand shoulder to shoulder with local political leaders and shower state resources on their jurisdictions. It gave the governor a stage to proclaim again his dedication to protecting the environment (thus contrasting himself with Sauerbrey) and to endear himself again to the environmental community.

Finally, it was an opportunity to do something the public clearly wanted the state to do: spend money to stop development, especially on the state's most scenic land. No matter that the amount of land that could be preserved through Rural Legacy easements was small compared to the amount threatened by sprawl, it was a start. Who wouldn't like the idea, the governor's aides thought, of the state buying development rights to protect the most beautiful, productive, historic, and economically significant rural lands in the state? Who would be opposed to that?

# Maryland Priority Funding Areas and Rural Legacy Lands

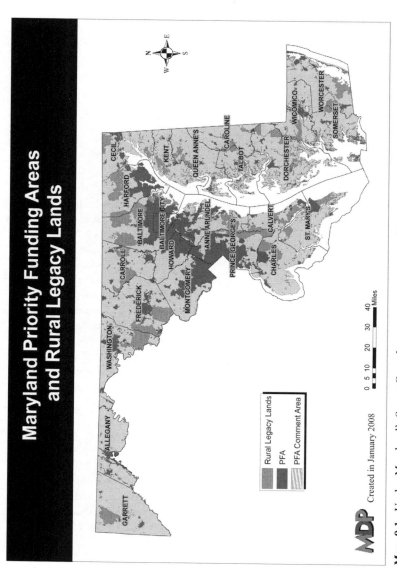

**Legend:**
- Rural Legacy Lands
- PFA
- PFA Comment Area

MDP  Created in January 2008

0 5 10   20   30   40 Miles

**Map 9.1.** Under Maryland's Smart Growth program, state expenditures for growth were generally restricted to Priority Funding Areas, while state expenditures for land preservation were targeted for designated Rural Legacy Areas.

The answer, of course, was that very few opposed using state funds to buy up development rights as a means of halting the spread of development. It was far more popular, for example, than any effort to increase development density within Priority Funding Areas. It was almost as if the public wanted to freeze development right where it was by *both* opposing higher densities in so-called "growth areas" while opposing new development in rural "protection areas." This phenomenon, hardly peculiar to Maryland, gave rise to the Smart Growth axiom that "there are only two things people don't like: one is density, the other is sprawl."

The public announcement of the first Rural Legacy awards was scheduled for June 1998, just five months before the election. By then, Glendening had shaken up his State House staff for the third time in eighteen months in search of someone who might arrest his general slide in popularity. The newest addition was a woman named Mara Gavin. Brought in to be a liaison between the State House staff and Glendening's campaign staff, Gavin knew little about Smart Growth or Rural Legacy and acted as if it was not important for her to learn. Her job was to make sure that whatever this announcement was, it would be heavily covered by the press. "How are we going to spin this, guys?" she would ask.

Most of the areas that were to be designated as the initial group of Rural Legacy recipients were, by definition, rural areas—out in the boonies and a long drive for Washington or Baltimore-based newspaper and television reporters to reach. The trick was to find an area that provided the scenic backdrop that would tell the story, but that was still close enough to the metropolitan areas to attract press coverage. The timing of press events is always critical: It has to be late enough to give reporters time to get to the event, but early enough for them to get back to write or edit their stories before the dinner hour. There was always the worry that a scheduled event could be trumped by a bigger unscheduled event—a plane crash, a lawsuit, an indictment or conviction, a death. Outdoor events added the uncertainty of inclement weather.

Gavin suggested the Rural Legacy event be held along the C&O Canal, in or near Washington, D.C., which she considered the news capital of the Free World. It didn't matter to her that none of the Rural Legacy areas were located anywhere near the Canal—what she was after was any sort of scenic backdrop and, more importantly, proximity to news reporters and TV cameras.

After an acrimonious fight over the location with Glendening's long-time staff, Gavin finally gave in to a site adjacent to a soon-to-be-designated Rural Legacy area in northern Montgomery County scouted and proposed by John Surrick, the able public relations man for the Department of Natural Resources. But Gavin made clear that if reporters failed to show up, if the event was a bust, or if it rained, we were all going to be in trouble.

On June 9, however, the weather was hot and clear when Parris Glendening strolled to the patio behind the rustic Comus Inn for the announcement. His backdrop was a plateau of farmland stretching to beautiful, oak-covered Sugarloaf Mountain on the Montgomery–Frederick County border in the distance. In front of him, arrayed in a semicircle, was a welcome site: a bank of eleven television cameras. Everybody would be happy.

If one announcement was good, then four would be great! The day after the Montgomery County event, the governor spoke at two additional Rural Legacy events, one next to a church in rural Baltimore County, the other on a river in Prince George's County. In two days, he carried the Rural Legacy message to the three most populous suburban jurisdictions in the state. He then traveled later in the week to Ocean City for a fourth announcement that would make news in Maryland's nine Eastern Shore counties. In all, he announced plans to spend $29 million as the state's first installment in Rural Legacy preservation. Sponsors that first year had sought more than $125 million to protect more than 53,000 acres, but Glendening urged patience, encouraging sponsors to try again next year. He said the state hoped to protect 200,000 acres by the year 2011 and, more importantly, to protect land at the same rate other lands were being developed.

At all four stops, the crowds were large and exuberant, the TV cameras abundant, the news coverage positive. For a governor who had been battered almost constantly for four years, this was a psychological lift. It had all the markings of a political lift as well.

## Living Jewel or Worst Example?

The issue that wouldn't go away, though, was Chapman's Landing.

When Glendening became the first Maryland governor ever to join the annual walk across the Chesapeake Bay Bridge in early May 1997, he was confronted with reminders of the Chapman's controversy everywhere he went. Environmentalists with "Save Chapman's Forest" bumper stickers glued to the backs of their jackets positioned themselves directly in front of Glendening and his entourage so he could not avoid seeing their message for most of the four-mile walk. School children who were accompanying Glendening were also pasted with the "Save Chapman's" bumper stickers until the increasingly irritated governor told an aide under his breath to have someone remove the signs from the kids.

By 1998, the election year pressure on Glendening to do something to stop the Chapman's development only intensified.

Finally, in August 1998, the state of Maryland, with the help of the non-profit Conservation Fund, agreed to pay Legend Development, Inc., the Virginia-based development company, $25.3 million to buy all but 375 acres of the 2,225-acre site.[9] The Chapman's Landing development had been stopped and the Chapman's Forest protected, but all at a huge cost to taxpayers. The price tag reflected the years of planning that had already gone into the project, which was so close to construction that at one point bulldozers had been brought to the site to begin clearing trees.

Reaction to the Chapman's purchase ranged from elation by environmentalists, who poured syrupy praise on Glendening; to outrage from a University of Maryland architect and Smart Growth supporter; to vilification from the head of the National Association of Home Builders.

"Governor Glendening, preserving Chapman's Forest will be a living jewel in your lasting legacy," gushed Joy Oakes, regional director of the Sierra Club.[10]

To Ralph Bennett, architect, proponent of New Urbanism, university professor and ardent supporter of Smart Growth, the purchase of Chapman's was "an unprincipled sellout." Contending that the houses that would have been built in Chapman's would be built elsewhere in Charles County anyway, but as sprawl rather than a well-planned development, Bennett said, "It dismisses in a stroke the hope that large parcels can be planned for both growth and conservation, while confirming our worst fears that Maryland will continue to fritter its open land away in unplanned, piecemeal, politically inconspicuous projects."[11]

Later that year at a national Smart Growth conference in Austin, Texas, Charles J. Ruma, a Columbus, Ohio, builder who then headed the NAHB, singled out the Chapman's Landing purchase in Maryland as the single worst example of so-called Smart Growth in the nation.

It didn't matter to Glendening what an Ohio builder thought; he was worried about what Maryland voters thought. In September, less than a month after the Chapman's purchase was announced, Glendening and his running mate, Lt. Gov. Kathleen Kennedy Townsend, won 70 percent of the vote in a four-way Democratic primary. Sauerbrey won 81 percent of the vote in a two-way Republican primary.

But their November faceoff would not be a repeat of the cliffhanger of four years earlier: Glendening, backed by environmentalists and Smart Growth advocates and benefiting from incumbency, handily won reelection by a 158,615-vote margin, 55 percent to 45 percent.

# Chapter 10

## Second Term Freedom

For those both inside and outside the administration, everything Glendening touched during his first term was seen through the prism of his bid for reelection—would it help him or hurt him? Did it position him to win, or make him vulnerable to attack? The governor was beset by a bad case of first-term political jitters, which sometimes sent him off on a course he otherwise would not have chosen. When Sauerbrey became a champion of cutting state taxes, for example, Glendening begrudgingly felt he had no choice but to respond with a tax cut of his own, albeit a much smaller one than his Republican opponent advocated. He hated it, but did it out of political self-defense.

By December 1998, however, Glendening seemed transformed. No longer worried about reelection, he was suddenly free to address issues in a second term that he really cared about, or which had been too controversial to try in a first term. Threat had vanished; opportunity had arrived. He had campaigned hard on environmental issues and as the Smart Growth candidate and now, confident and finally comfortable in his position as governor, he believed he had a mandate from the people to pursue those goals.

Buoyed by his ten percentage point margin of victory, Glendening met with his cabinet secretaries and staff and told them he wanted to demonstrate how serious he was about Smart Growth. He said he wanted to show that for state government, it would no longer be "business as usual." To achieve "Smart Growth," he said, the state would have to do things differently. He directed his cabinet secretaries to review their budgets and programs to ensure that everything they were proposing was consistent not only with the Smart Growth law, but with its spirit as well. He said if there were projects that would have moved forward in the past but which now must be stopped because they were inconsistent with Smart Growth, he wanted to make examples of them. He said he wanted to prove to the public that he was serious about changing the culture.[1]

## Neighborhood Conservation

As his second term was about to begin, the governor replaced two key members of his cabinet, Housing Secretary Patricia Payne and Transportation Secretary David Winstead. Asked by reporters to explain the changes, Glendening said neither had been strong enough supporters of the Smart Growth effort. In reality, the two were almost certainly pushed out for other, unrelated reasons. Payne, in particular, had worked hard on Smart Growth projects and Winstead was trying to get the lumbering Department of Transportation to be more responsive. But the way the story was reported in the state's newspapers had the effect Glendening wanted. Suddenly, other cabinet secretaries began showing up at Smart Growth Sub-Cabinet meetings to which they had previously sent surrogates.

To replace Winstead at the Maryland Department of Transportation, Glendening picked a longtime confidant and loyal assistant, John D. Porcari. One of the smartest and most competent members of Glendening's staff, Porcari had worked for Glendening in Prince George's County and accompanied him to Annapolis in 1995. He initially served as the governor's personal negotiator on economic development deals back when Glendening viewed himself as "the economic development governor."

"When John Porcari speaks," Glendening told members of his cabinet at their very first meeting in 1995, "it is as if I am speaking."[2] Later in the first term, however, Porcari left state government for a job with Loiderman Soltesz Associates, a development engineering firm, only to be lured back by Glendening to become Winstead's deputy at MDOT. To insiders, it seemed obvious that it was only a matter of time until Winstead would be pushed aside and Porcari appointed to take his place.

The trait Porcari brought to the job that Winstead sometimes lacked was an ability to understand exactly what Glendening wanted done. The Department of Transportation had a budget that exceeded $2 billion a year and both Glendening and Porcari understood that this huge pot of money could be used to support the Smart Growth initiative. They knew that nothing drove development decisions more than where the state decided to invest funds for highway construction or expansion or to build transit lines.

Glendening's "transportation vision started with transit," Porcari later recalled.[3] He wanted to change the balance, change the funding ratio between highways and transit. Most of this was really very conceptual—a thirty-thousand-foot conversation we were having."

Porcari said he tried to translate that concept into specific action, developing a statewide transportation plan that was more balanced between highways and transit, a goal of doubling transit ridership by 2020, an attempt to encourage diehard highway engineers to start planning for bikeways and hiking paths, and to force the Washington Metropolitan

**Fig. 10.1.** U.S. Senator Paul Sarbanes (left), Glendening and Transportation Secretary John D. Porcari supported an increase in transit projects as part of Maryland's Smart Growth effort. Photo courtesy of the *Baltimore Sun*.

Area Transit Authority to work collaboratively for the first time with Maryland's Mass Transit Administration.

Glendening, Porcari recalled, "was pretty blunt in saying he thought MDOT was one of the most retrograde agencies around—that it supported a bunch of fat old white boys getting rich on highway contracts. And there was some reality to that."[4]

To overcome this perception and respond to the governor's concept of what a transportation department should be doing in a Smart Growth context, Porcari and his state highway administrator, Parker Williams, devised a program called Neighborhood Conservation. The idea was to use funds that in previous years might have been earmarked for highway construction and expansion projects instead to revitalize state roads that ran through the center of small Maryland towns and cities. In most instances, other than periodic resurfacing, these roads had not been improved since they were first built, yet they ran right through the centers of towns all over the state.

With funds from the Neighborhood Conservation program, concrete slab sidewalks could be replaced by bricks, trees planted and landscaping added, ornamental lights and park benches installed, and neighboring businesses coerced into improving their building facades in exchange for receiving the state help. It was all intended to make older downtown business districts more attractive places to live or shop and to do so at a relatively low cost.

"We asked ourselves, 'Who has been paying into the Transportation Trust Fund and not getting anything back?' The answer was older urban neighborhoods. They were receiving no attention other than occasional repaving. They weren't even getting much in the way of bus service," said Porcari, explaining the politics behind the program. "It was a basic equity issue—who paid and who got the services. The argument was that we were only subsidizing the suburbs—they were the only ones who were getting new roads and the only ones with new service.[5]

"Of course, in the big three jurisdictions [Baltimore City and Montgomery and Prince George's counties] this meshed with Parris's political base."[6]

Rather than starting there, however, MDOT intentionally initiated the Neighborhood Conservation Program in several small, rural communities, including in the home districts of some of the General Assembly's powerful committee chairmen. "They went from potentially being the biggest enemies of this to the guys who said, 'This is something I can deliver. I'm not going to get an I-68 in my lifetime, but I'm going to get a Neighborhood Conservation project in a period of four years,'" Porcari said.[7]

"We could explicitly say: We're going to design it, you're going to turn the shovel and you're going to cut a ribbon before you run for reelection," Porcari explained. "Suddenly, you don't need a seventy million dollar highway interchange—you need a two point five million dollar Neighborhood Conservation project."[8]

As a result of this work, both Williams and his director of planning, Neil Pedersen, became national leaders within the American Association of State Highway and Transportation Officials (AASHTO) for their "context sensitive design" work, which they cleverly named "Thinking Beyond the Pavement." From the Smart Growth perspective, transportation in general and highway work in particular could suddenly be blended with the efforts of other state agencies working on housing, park development, or environmental protection.

"Maryland went from what was always one of the best highway departments in the country to this much more comprehensive approach and Parker and Neil got a lot of recognition professionally," Porcari said. "I think they got a lot of satisfaction out of it."[9]

## Five Bypasses

One of the first Smart Growth actions to garner Porcari's attention, however, was not a decision to build a new road, but rather a decision *not* to build five new roads.

Following the governor's instructions to screen projects for consistency with Smart Growth, the Department of Transportation reviewed every project in its six-year capital construction program and identified five proposed highway bypass projects* that failed the Smart Growth test. The Smart Growth law said that money for highways could only be expended if a new road was completely within a Priority Funding Area or if it connected Priority Funding Areas. There were exceptions for roads that needed to be built because of safety reasons, or to connect to some activity that by its very nature was outside of a PFA, such as a state park or a mining operation, or for which certain approvals had already been granted at the time the legislation was enacted.

But the proposed alignments for these five highway bypass projects failed the test. They were generally outside of PFA boundaries, they did not connect PFAs, and there were no special reasons why they should be built. The state's Smart Growth concern was that the bypasses would merely promote more sprawl in rural or lightly developed areas.

The bypasses were generally considered high cost, low priority projects included in the long-range plan primarily to mollify local elected officials. There was little likelihood any of them would be built anytime soon, if ever.

---

*The proposed bypass projects were to be located in Westminster and Manchester in Carroll County, Chestertown connecting Kent and Queen Anne's counties, Lonaconing in Allegany County, and Brookeville in Montgomery County.

"We had a number of internal discussions about it within MDOT before we brought the draft CTP [six-year Consolidated Transportation Plan] to [Glendening]. I came to the conclusion that we had to take the bypasses out of the program. They were never going to be built. They were out in Year Six and always would be, so there was no political downside in leaving them there. But, technically you couldn't check off the 'Smart Growth box' on any of them."[10]

Consistent with Glendening's desire to make examples of projects that did not conform to the Smart Growth initiative, MDOT planned to announce that the bypasses had been removed from the long-range plan and explain why. At the last moment, however, a decision was made not to draw attention to the bypass decision because it might also draw attention to a modest revenue increase proposed elsewhere within the overall transportation plan to be unveiled that January. There was a futile hope within MDOT that if the cancelled bypasses weren't highlighted, maybe it wouldn't cause that much of a stir. From a public relations standpoint, that turned out to be a serious mistake.

When local officials, particularly those from Carroll and Montgomery counties, reviewed the new six-year plan and discovered that their bypass projects had been eliminated without their knowledge or consultation, they threw a fit.

"That was fairly ugly," Porcari later remembered. "There were more fireworks than I anticipated."[11]

Projects that had never risen higher than the sixth year of a rolling six-year construction plan suddenly were embraced as if the first shovel of dirt was about to be turned. Killing the bypasses turned the projects into martyrs—slain by the cruel heavy hand of Smart Growth. Glendening announced that planning money for the five bypasses would be used, instead, to find alternative solutions to the traffic problems that gave rise to the projects in the first place. But residents living near the cancelled projects generally said they just wanted their bypass projects restored and someday built.

The dispute over these highways festered off and on for nearly two years. Teams from the governor's office and MDOT visited each community, explained the decision, and tried to work out compromises. The most vehement opposition came from Manchester in Carroll County and Brookeville in Montgomery County.

In heavily Republican Carroll County, where two of the five axed projects were to have been built, the decision was cast as a blatantly partisan attack by the Democratic governor. Porcari said the internal discussions at MDOT focused on who would use the proposed bypasses, not the political affiliation of residents. "I remember a big part of our internal discussion was that a lot of those commuters [in Carroll County] were from Pennsylvania. So, the question was, 'We're doing this for what? For Pennsylvania commuters?'"[12]

State highway engineers developed a substitute plan to substantially improve the flow of traffic on Route 30 through Manchester, but local officials rejected the effort, fearing acceptance would mean they would never get their bypass built.

That's when two state officials who served on the Board of Public Works with Glendening got involved. Maryland's Board of Public Works generally passes judgment on state contracts, but it also is empowered to vote on project exemptions from the state's Smart Growth law. State Treasurer Richard Dixon was from Carroll County, so his motive in the Manchester issue was clear. The state comptroller, former governor William Donald Schaefer, simply relished any opportunity to stick it to Glendening. On a 2–1 vote, they teamed together to demand that the Manchester project be restored to MDOT's long-range transportation program.

Undeterred, Glendening asked the state attorney general if having the project exempted meant he had to provide funding to build it. The attorney general subsequently issued an opinion that said it remained the governor's prerogative whether to fund projects listed in the transportation construction program. Glendening then sealed the issue by saying he had no intention of budgeting money for the Manchester bypass.

In Montgomery County, where nonstop, rush hour traffic poured through the quaint, historic community of Brookeville on its way to Washington each morning and on the way back home each evening, residents simply wanted relief so they could cross the street in safety.

When highway engineers visited Brookeville, they suggested several ways to speed traffic along narrow Route 97, which zigzags through the town and eventually turns into busy Georgia Avenue, a major thoroughfare into and out of Washington. The problem was that Route 97 could not be straightened because it runs so close to the front of historic buildings. Many of these same, stately brick buildings were already there on August 24, 1814, when President James Madison fled a burning Washington and sought refuge with his friend Caleb Bentley, the first postmaster of Brookeville. For one day, Brookeville claimed the title: "Capital of the United States."

"You don't understand," one resident told the highway engineers. "We don't want to speed up traffic; we want to slow it down." Traffic, the residents said, was killing their town. They demanded to know how cancellation of a bypass designed to protect the historic town could possibly be construed as "Smart Growth."[13]

Resolution of the Brookeville problem resulted in one of the most unique and unorthodox highway projects ever developed by the state. In a deal secretly negotiated by Gene Lynch, then Glendening's deputy chief of staff, the state and Montgomery County agreed to restore the Brookeville bypass to MDOT's six-year plan, but in such a way as to minimize the road's ability to generate more sprawl development. The two

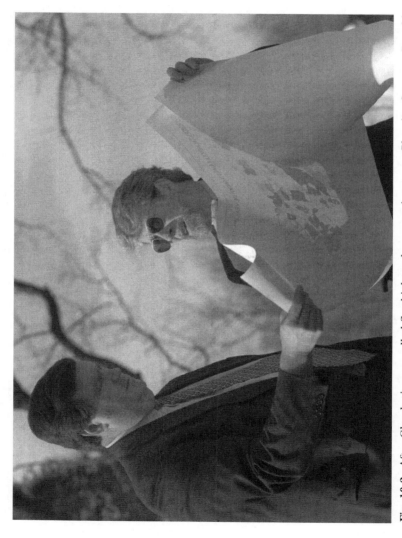

**Fig. 10.2.** After Glendening cancelled five highway bypass projects, state Planning Secretary Ronald Kreitner (right) had to explain the decision on the Brookeville Bypass to Montgomery County Executive Doug Duncan. Photo courtesy of the *Baltimore Sun.*

sides agreed that whenever the bypass is finally built, it would remain two lanes wide (like the roads connecting to it north and south) and feature traffic-slowing roundabouts at the northern and southern ends. One of the most novel ideas was that narrow easements would be placed along both sides of the road to assure that no new development or connections to other roads would be permitted along its path. Finally, if all of that failed to prevent the new road from generating a large increase in traffic, then Montgomery County agreed it would reimburse the state in full for the cost of the project.

Lynch's deal defused a potentially ugly political fight with Montgomery County, which had generally been supportive of Glendening and his Smart Growth efforts.

## The Sidewalk on Route 202

Porcari traces the transformation in thinking within the Maryland Department of Transportation to an incident that actually started back when Glendening was still the Prince George's County executive and which carried over into his first-term appointments.

Glendening had noticed a dirt walking path that connected a public housing complex with a nearby grocery store along Route 202, a state highway that ran through Prince George's County. Glendening, Porcari remembered, asked Hal Kasoff, then the state highway administrator, to fix the problem, but Kasoff informed the county executive that the state had a policy of not retrofitting existing roads with new sidewalks. After Glendening became governor, he repeated the request to Kasoff and Kasoff repeated his answer. Soon thereafter, Kasoff was looking for a new job and Parker Williams was subsequently hired to replace him.[14]

To hammer home the point with SHA, Glendening then introduced legislation that established a $3 million sidewalk program that, in part, was to be used to build new sidewalks along existing state highways.

The sidewalk program was later broadened to become the Neighborhood Conservation program.

## Pressing Forward

For the remainder of Glendening's second term, he and his staff steadily pressed forward with the Smart Growth initiative. Efforts were made to make the state's brownfield cleanup law more efficient. Responsibility for brownfield cleanup and redevelopment was split between two state agencies, a remnant of the 1996 and 1997 political fight between business interests and environmentalists. When would-be developers protested that it was too costly to conduct initial assessments of suspected brownfield sites to determine how badly they might be contaminated, Glendening agreed that the state should help cover the cost.*

When it became obvious that Maryland's historic preservation tax credit was becoming one of the most effective of all Smart Growth incentives, the General Assembly agreed to increase the percentage of tax credit developers could claim, first from 10 percent to 15 percent in 1997, then to 25 percent just a year later to spur even more redevelopment activity.[15] (Subsequently, the General Assembly in 2001 reduced this tax credit to 20 percent, capped the amount the state would pay for projects in a given year, and placed other constraints on the program, all to the dismay of Smart Growth proponents.)

The governor took particular interest in efforts to renovate historic theaters around the state, such as the Silver Theater in Silver Spring† or the Hippodrome, a once popular vaudeville theater in downtown Baltimore, both of which had been closed and abandoned. More than $60 million in state, city, and private funds were poured into renovating the Hippodrome, turning it into a Broadway quality theater and anchor project for a comprehensive redevelopment of the west side of downtown Baltimore. This redevelopment effort was being managed by Westside Renaissance, a nonprofit organization created by a coalition of Baltimore businesses and headed by Kreitner, Glendening's former planning secretary.

On the land preservation side, the state continued to award millions of dollars in new Rural Legacy grants each year, steadily expanding the amount of land protected from spreading development. At Glendening's behest, staff at the Department of Agriculture and Department of Natural Resources began looking for opportunities to use the state's farmland preservation and parkland acquisition funds to augment Rural Legacy purchases. The Department of Natural Resources conducted an inventory of the state's remaining ecologically significant lands and developed a new land preservation program, called GreenPrint, designed specifically to protect lands of special environmental value.

As he neared the end of his term, Glendening became more forceful in using Rural Legacy funds as a reward to counties that had moved expeditiously to acquire the development rights on threatened properties and began withholding Rural Legacy funds as a way of penalizing counties that did not.

---

*Despite the procedural improvements, the brownfields program suffered from a chronic shortage of money that could be used as incentives to entice developers to build on the reclaimed properties.

†As a result of this renovation, the Silver Theater became the national home of the American Film Institute.

The administration made several high-profile land purchases, among them: Belt Woods, an old-growth forest in Prince George's County; Deep Creek Lake, a recreational lake in Garrett County originally built and owned by a Pennsylvania power company; and, the Smith farm, a relic of Howard County's agricultural past that had become surrounded by the "new town" of Columbia.

## The *National* Center for Smart Growth

In 1999, James R. Cohen, a professor in the University of Maryland's Urban Studies and Planning Program, convinced his colleagues that the university should take advantage of the exploding interest in Smart Growth by establishing a Smart Growth research and education center at the College Park campus. The group of professors decided to seek money to do this from a competitive enhancement fund the university had established to encourage the creation of innovative programs.

While this proposal was pending, Cohen, Tom Kennedy, who headed the School of Public Affairs' Executive Programs office, and his assistant, Tracy Stanton, drove to Baltimore to float the idea with Deputy Planning Secretary Ron Young and Frece, the governor's assistant for Smart Growth. They outlined their concept for a Smart Growth Center that they said would be affiliated with six schools or programs: the Department of Civil Engineering; the Urban Studies and Planning Program; the School of Architecture; the School of Public Affairs; the Department of Agricultural and Resource Economics; and the Department of Natural Resource Sciences and Landscape Architecture.* He said a request for slightly more than $600,000 had already been made to the university and asked if Glendening and the state would be supportive.

Both Young and Frece were enthusiastic about the idea, but Young told the university team they weren't thinking big enough—this shouldn't just be a Center for Smart Growth, Young insisted; it should be the *National* Center for Smart Growth.[16] The group discussed how the center might become a national resource on Smart Growth issues, a repository of information about growth management, a center for serious research on land use efforts, and a focal point for education and training for local, state, and even federal officials about Smart Growth goals, policies, and strategies.

University officials also liked the concept, but only provided $350,000 of the $600,000 requested. Learning of this in February 2000, Frece proposed to Glendening that he fill the gap by asking the General Assembly

---

*The center was ultimately affiliated with four schools: the School of Engineering; the College of Agricultural and Natural Resources; the renamed School of Architecture, Planning and Preservation; and the renamed School of Public Policy.

to appropriate $400,000 for the National Center for Smart Growth Education and Research as part of the supplemental budget he was planning to submit toward the end of the 2000 legislative session.[17] The governor readily agreed.

Legislators, particularly Senate Budget and Taxation Committee Chairwoman Barbara Hoffman of Baltimore, however, were not happy to be asked at the end of a legislative session to fund a new university research center they had never heard of and for which they had no time to hold hearings. Once again, however, the lawmakers understood this proposal was connected to Glendening's number one issue, so they begrudgingly approved it, but only after cutting the appropriation in half to $200,000.

That summer, the National Center for Smart Growth Research and Education started slowly, with a small staff and few resources, but by 2007 it had recruited a staff of eight, including six full-time research faculty, plus two dozen affiliated faculty, and had attracted more than $4 million in research grants. Researchers and grad assistants were working on Maryland-specific projects (such as assessing housing trends or the implementation of adequate public facilities ordinances), on projects in a half-dozen major metropolitan areas around the country, and on projects or programs in both China and Europe.

In 2005 and 2006, the center became a lead sponsor for a series of public growth visioning exercises (known by the name of "Reality Check") held in Washington, D.C., Fredericksburg, Va., and in four regions covering the entire state of Maryland. For the remainder of the Glendening years, the center also offered a popular Smart Growth Leadership course that brought together municipal, county, state, and sometimes federal officials and private sector representatives to discuss Smart Growth strategies, goals, and obstacles.

## Smart Codes

While the land preservation efforts were booming, efforts to spur redevelopment in older communities were frequently stymied by state and local codes—zoning, building, rehabilitation, and even fire protection codes—that made it almost impossible to build the kinds of communities Smart Growth advocates envisioned. In speeches, Glendening started showing a photograph of downtown Annapolis and telling audiences that even though it was one of the most popular destinations in the state—historic, mixed use, walkable, scenic, and possessing a unique "sense of place"—it would be illegal to build a new Annapolis under current zoning or building codes.

To focus attention on the problem, the governor hosted a "Smart Codes" conference in Baltimore in May 1999. It attracted several hundred builders, code enforcement officials, developers, Smart Growth and housing advocates, an array of state officials, and various top fire department officials. Oddly, in many localities it was the fire prevention officials who opposed code changes that would permit narrower streets, mixed uses in the same buildings, and other changes sought in the name of Smart Growth. Often they complained their fire trucks would not have room to maneuver or the risk of fatalities from fires would be increased by permitting mixes of uses in the same building.

When Glendening's car pulled up outside the Smart Codes conference and the governor stepped to the curb, he was greeted by several aides and the state fire marshal, Rocco J. Gabrielle. Without so much as a "Hello," Glendening looked at Gabrielle and said, "I hear you're part of the problem." The surprised Gabrielle paused for a split second and then replied, "Not anymore."[18]

A task force formed as the result of the conference later recommended that the state completely revise its building rehabilitation code much in the way New Jersey had done with great success a year earlier. It also recommended that the state draft model codes to encourage and assist local governments with infill and other mixed use redevelopment projects. The Governor could have simply directed his Department of Planning* to draft the model codes, but to imbue the effort with broader authority he instead asked for General Assembly approval. But in this effort, like so many before it, the state once again shied away from trying to impose zoning or other code requirements on local governments, offering only to provide model codes as a form of technical assistance.

In his next-to-last year in office, Glendening pushed through one additional program aimed at jump-starting revitalization projects. Designed largely by Ellen Janes, an assistant secretary for redevelopment within the Department of Housing and Community Development, the new "Community Legacy" program was modeled in many ways after the successful Rural Legacy program. The concept behind the two programs was the same: the state would put up a pot of money each year and citizen groups could compete for a share to be used for their projects. The amounts of money available through the Community Legacy program were far smaller than those available for Rural Legacy lands and the eligible uses, of course, were completely different. Community Legacy funds were to be used by community groups or other project sponsors to pay for the demolition of useless or derelict buildings or to finance other specific redevelopment activities that could not be paid for with funds from other more categorical

---

*During the 2000 Maryland General Assembly session, Glendening sought and received legislative approval to upgrade the Office of Planning to cabinet rank, saying that renaming it the Department of Planning better reflected its important role as the lead agency for Smart Growth.

state programs. The importance of the Community Legacy program was that it would provide flexible funding for work not covered by any other "categorical" program.

Piece by piece, year by year, Glendening and his staff added to the Smart Growth program, expanded it, tossed in more money, and tried to fill gaps. Every major department had a staff person responsible for coordinating Smart Growth activities. Most cabinet secretaries became regular participants in cross-departmental projects and most sent their staff to the University of Maryland's Smart Growth training sessions.

Staff to the governor, working with the Department of Planning, relentlessly packaged it all for public consumption, producing pamphlets and technical guidebooks, preparing speeches and Power Point presentations, and both seeking and giving out awards and recognition.

Gradually, Smart Growth became the basic framework for state government activities, from decisions on highway construction to housing assistance to land preservation.

# Chapter 11

# Clicking on All Cylinders

Governor Parris N. Glendening strode confidently across the lobby of the historic Hotel Del Coronado. He had just delivered a luncheon keynote address to hundreds gathered in sunny San Diego for a national Smart Growth conference and the governor was riding high. One after another, conference attendees stopped him to say how inspirational he had been or how the Maryland example had made it possible for them to work on Smart Growth issues in their home state. The governor seemed to savor each compliment, each new pat on the back, as his reward for pushing the Smart Growth initiative so hard.

An aide, joining the governor for a post-luncheon cup of coffee, sought to capitalize on the moment. Back home, the University of Maryland wanted to build a new satellite campus in Western Maryland on the rural outskirts of the city of Hagerstown. The county seat of Washington County, Hagerstown dated to before the American Revolution. By the Civil War, it had become a major railroad junction and was raided by Confederate General Jubal Early. In more recent years, however, as houses and stores were developed on the city's fringe, the city's economy suffered and its downtown, like that in many other older communities, declined.

While the site proposed for the new University of Maryland campus was just inside the edge of the city's Priority Funding Area and therefore technically in compliance with the Smart Growth law, it was far from downtown, was not served by utilities, was distant from city police and fire services, and was reachable only by car. The location would do little for the struggling city. The plan was legal, but it was counter to the Smart Growth Executive Order that required state agencies to give priority to downtown business districts. More troubling from the political perspective, it was contrary to the spirit of the Smart Growth law. How would the "Smart Growth governor" explain such a decision?

Hagerstown's mayor had a better idea. He wanted the new campus to be located in Baldwin House, a historic but abandoned hotel attached to an abandoned department store a half block from the town's main square. Inside, the dilapidated building was a shambles, with a leaking roof, rotting floors, and crumbling plaster. It had been uninhabited for twenty years or longer.

The handsome exterior façade was tired, but still intact enough to serve as the anchor to Hagerstown's historic preservation district. Although Glendening readily understood that the downtown site was preferable from a Smart Growth perspective, there were concerns that the redevelopment costs might be much higher than the cost of building outside of town. Glendening had been inexplicably slow in deciding what the university should do. To the governor's staff, it was unclear whether it was due to the project's potential cost or the heated local political opposition to putting the campus downtown.

The university itself had acted as if it were unaware that Maryland had a Smart Growth law or an executive order that mandated state agencies to give preference to downtown business districts when locating new facilities. Even though the university's School of Public Affairs was then teaching its Smart Growth course, university officials had to be dragged to a faceoff with Department of Planning officials who demanded to know why the university was so opposed to the downtown location. Their response included concerns about the potentially higher cost of renovating than building new, whether sufficient parking would be available, or whether night students would go to a campus downtown where there might be a fear of crime.

But back in California, with the compliments from the conference attendees still ringing in the governor's ears, the aide pressed for a decision.

After a short discussion, the governor suddenly decided. "It needs to go downtown," he said, and instructed the aide to call the State House in Annapolis right away to order up a press release explaining the governor's decision.[1]

This was a lesson both in Smart Growth decision making and in personal motivation. It demonstrated one of the weaknesses in the Priority Funding Area designation by clearly showing that all locations within a PFA were not necessarily equal from a Smart Growth perspective. On the personal level, it seemed that the more Glendening did to advance Smart Growth, the more accolades he received. And, the more accolades he received, the more eager he was to advance Smart Growth.

The downtown campus in Hagerstown has been a success. Just as critics feared, the final renovation cost (about $13 million plus another $2 million to develop an adjacent lot into a downtown campus park) exceeded the $11.5 million estimate for the somewhat smaller building originally envisioned on a cow pasture on the edge of town near Interstate 70. But any visitor to downtown Hagerstown can see the spinoff effect of this facility, with new shops and restaurants popping up in surrounding

**Fig. 11.1.** The "Baldwin House" was an abandoned and deteriorating former hotel and department store at the time it was offered for free to the state as a potential site for a new University of Maryland satellite campus in Hagerstown.

**Fig. 11.2.** Restored to its historic appearance in the front, and with a large modern wing added to the back, the new University of Maryland campus in Hagerstown now offers a variety of courses and has spurred redevelopment in the nearby downtown area.

blocks. Pedestrian traffic has picked up, perhaps a tribute to the police substation installed on the campus building's ground floor. The old hotel and department store were renovated with historic accuracy, but a modern new building with a several-story atrium was attached to the rear of the building to provide new classroom space. In all, the 77,000 square foot campus houses forty-four offices, twenty-four classrooms, a library and computer lab, and offers programs in education, business, social work, nursing, and other subjects by the University of Maryland, Frostburg University, and the University of Maryland at Baltimore. When the doors opened on January 24, 2005, 527 students were enrolled, almost all of whom were night students who could park in the adjacent city garage that had been mostly vacant at night before the campus was completed.

## A National Tour

By the end of his term, Glendening had become a regular on the national Smart Growth lecture circuit. He barnstormed through California, Oregon, Washington, and South Carolina, and in St. Louis, Chicago, and Miami. He spoke before housing groups, historic preservation groups, land preservation groups, and business groups. He even talked about Smart Growth on his economic development missions abroad.

In a meeting arranged by Jane Nishida, his secretary of environment, Glendening took his Smart Growth message to the first joint conference of state environmental and transportation secretaries held in Atlanta. He promoted Smart Growth side by side with Republican Governor Mike Leavitt of Utah, Democratic Governor Roy Barnes of Georgia, and Independent Governor Jesse Ventura of Minnesota.

As chairman of the National Governors' Association's Natural Resources Committee, he succeeded in gaining NGA endorsement of "10 Principles of Smart Growth."[2] In July 2000, when he became chairman of the NGA, his "chairman's initiative" for the year was "Quality Growth,"* and the NGA staff subsequently produced a series of well-regarded reports on growth pressures and state responses around the nation. His tenure as chairman ended at the summer meeting in Providence, Rhode Island, a city on the upswing after Smart Growth–style revitalization had rejuvenated the city, uncovering its once decked-over river and moving a huge train yard that had marred the view from the front of the state capital in the center of the city.

---

*The phrase "Quality Growth" was considered more politically acceptable than "Smart Growth," particularly to Republican governors who then controlled the NGA and who linked the "Smart Growth" tag not only to Glendening, but also to Democratic presidential candidate Al Gore.

The machinery of Smart Growth in Maryland was clicking on all cylinders. In October 2000, Maryland's Smart Growth initiative was awarded $100,000 as one of ten winners of the annual *Innovations in American Government* awards program co-sponsored by Harvard University, the Ford Foundation, and the Council for Excellence in Government. While the money was helpful, it was the recognition—and bragging rights—that meant the most to Glendening and his Smart Growth team. From the initiative's earliest days, part of the strategy of the governor's staff had been to seek outside recognition because it inevitably made it easier to sell the product at home.

## A Change at Planning

Earlier that same year, Ron Kreitner, the longtime state planning director and secretary, announced plans to take another job as head of a nonprofit organization overseeing the redevelopment of the west side of downtown Baltimore. Kreitner had been a voice in support of Smart Growth since long before the concept was even called Smart Growth. He was the senior member of the Glendening cabinet and had headed the planning department for more than eleven years, longer than any of his predecessors.

Though he clearly knew his subject, Kreitner's quiet, low-key style never quite satisfied Glendening, who periodically complained behind Kreitner's back that he wanted someone more aggressive and forceful to lead his Smart Growth effort. But it had been Kreitner who supplied much of the brain power behind the effort, backing up the governor's proposals and strategies with research, statistics, maps, sound planning, and an insightful understanding of the politics of Smart Growth. He knew and understood local planners better than just about anyone in state government. And no one was better than Kreitner in understanding how various state agencies could or should work together to make Smart Growth projects happen.

As he was about to walk out the door, Kreitner gave Glendening an unexpected recommendation for his replacement: Harriet Tregoning. Tregoning wasn't a planner, but rather was trained in engineering and public policy and had spent nearly two decades in the field of environmental protection. She directed an office within the U.S. Environmental Protection Agency[3] that, in 1997, had started a network of more than two dozen national organizations interested in Smart Growth. Maryland had been a charter member (and the only partner that represented a state government) of the original Smart Growth Network, but Glendening did not know her. Yet, he was intrigued by her resume (sent to him by Kreitner) and invited Tregoning for an interview.

From the governor's perspective, the prospect of hiring Tregoning was inspired: here was someone with a national perspective on Smart Growth just as Glendening was about to let the issue carry him onto the national stage. While she lacked Kreitner's planning credentials and was a neophyte to Maryland politics, she was a quick learner and an adept political strategist. Moreover, she possessed some of the personal leadership skills Glendening wanted. She would never be described as "quiet and low-key."

In July 2000, Tregoning became the state's first new planning secretary in a dozen years. She arrived at her new office in Baltimore with fresh ideas, a couple of hand-picked staff assistants, and the enthusiasm of someone who had talked about Smart Growth in theory for years and now had an opportunity to put the theory into practice. Her goal was to get the state to do a better job linking transportation, land use, and housing policies.

## The Office of Smart Growth

Glendening seemed enthusiastic and pleased with Tregoning's performance at Planning. Yet, within six months, the governor came up with a new idea: he wanted to establish an entirely new Office of Smart Growth within the governor's office. It was unclear who would head such an office, although Glendening had a long and dispiriting penchant for trumping his own appointments by bringing in someone new in a slightly more powerful position.

Both Tregoning and Frece worried that the new Office of Smart Growth could rob them of any authority on Smart Growth issues or, worse, render their respective positions meaningless. Tregoning wondered privately why she was there if she wasn't going to lead the Smart Growth effort? Frece knew that at least two people outside of state government had approached Glendening about being hired to lead the Smart Growth effort and suspected there were others. Whatever the task, Glendening always seemed to be searching for someone new, someone who might have the magic bullet, someone whose hiring alone might buy him a little positive ink until the next best thing came along.

There also was concern that legislators would see the proposal as creating an unnecessary new and costly layer of bureaucracy—just the kind of political target the Smart Growth program had cleverly avoided up until then. The legislature liked to slap down empire builders and it seemed to some of the governor's top aides that he was setting himself—and Smart Growth—up for a fall.

### Sabotage

In December, Frece was asked his opinion of the proposal by Jennifer Crawford, a young staff assistant whom Glendening had recently promoted to deputy chief of staff and put in charge of Smart Growth.

"You asked that I take a look at your initial attempt to describe the appropriate functions for the proposed Governor's Office on Smart

Growth and help re-draft it in a way that makes more sense within the context of the Smart Growth initiative," Frece wrote in an eight-page memo to Crawford on December 20, 2000.[4] He went on to lay out two options for the new office: "(1) A 'super agency,' with broad oversight over the entire Smart Growth initiative; or, (2) a more focused, more practical 'one-stop-shop' for helping to implement Smart Growth on the ground." He recommended the second option.

"I firmly believe this more project-oriented approach will result in an office that not only meets a real world need, but would undoubtedly be less confusing (and therefore more acceptable) to the legislature, the general public and even to the Governor's Cabinet in terms of chain of command for Smart Growth decision-making."

Only months before, during the 2000 legislative session, Frece noted, the governor "convinced the legislature to elevate the Office of Planning to department status precisely because of its lead role in implementing the Smart Growth initiative." He also pointed out that just six months earlier Tregoning had been hired and said, "I am fearful that this new office, if it is not structured carefully, could inadvertently undermine her authority and thus reduce her effectiveness."[5]

The memo suggested that "Option 2" would accomplish the governor's goal of institutionalizing the Smart Growth program, but in a way that would be "much less intimidating to counties and other local government officials that have feared from the outset the creation of a 'state land use czar.'[6]

"Keep in mind," the memo concluded, "Maryland is already widely considered the leader in the country on these issues, so the folks in our cabinet who are working on these programs must be doing something right. Why superimpose another level of bureaucracy on top of a governmental structure that clearly has been successful and which shows no signs of slowing down? What we really need is help in getting good examples of Smart Growth out of the ground. That will be more important than anything else we can do in changing public opinion."[7]

Frece sent the memo to Crawford and went home for the Christmas holidays. Several days later, however, he received a call saying the governor wanted to see him in his office a day or two after Christmas. In the governor's State House office, Frece pulled up a chair directly in front of the governor's desk and took a seat. Glendening, quietly angry, held up the memo and demanded to know, "What are you trying to do? Sabotage me?"[8]

Crawford clearly had handed the memo directly to the governor, who apparently was offended that his idea for this new superagency had been questioned and, just as importantly, worried that a copy of such a candid memo could fall into the hands of the press or one of his political opponents. The meeting, which was mostly a one-sided conversation, ended with the governor saying he was moving ahead with his plans for the Office of Smart Growth and expected his staff to be on board as well.

Begrudgingly, the General Assembly once again acceded to the governor's wishes and approved the creation of the Office of Smart Growth. As some on Glendening's staff predicted, there was a lot of grumbling by legislators about duplicate layers of bureaucracy, unnecessary expense, confusing chains of command, and so on. But legislative leaders also knew Smart Growth had become the governor's number one issue, so they were not about to cross him over such a relatively minor expenditure. It was not worth the retribution the governor would inflict in retaliation.

## Intervention

In July 2001, the Office of Smart Growth opened for business. By then, Glendening had publicly announced that he was moving Tregoning from planning to become the state's first Special Secretary for Smart Growth. Frece became the office's communications director.

At first, the office was spread between locations in Baltimore and Annapolis. Glendening insisted that Frece move from his office from the Department of Natural Resources a half mile away to an office on the second floor of the State House just so the governor could say that the Office of Smart Growth was so important to him that it was located just steps from his own office. Eventually, the OSG staff consolidated in larger quarters in a state-owned office building directly across the street from the State House.

Tregoning was a dynamo. With the governor's approval, she borrowed talented people from the Department of Transportation, the Department of Environment, the Department of Natural Resources, the Department of Planning and elsewhere within state government to staff the new Office of Smart Growth. She and her chief of staff, Jessica Cogan, finagled office space and sweet-talked or bullied cabinet secretaries into giving the office desks, computers, and other resources. Together, Tregoning and Cogan—with Glendening's tacit approval—coerced other cabinet secretaries to give up top staff or vacant positions so the new special secretary for Smart Growth could fill those vacancies with fresh outside hires. Tregoning and Cogan even convinced the Maryland Higher Education Commission to designate two of the four Governor's Policy Fellows that the state hired each year specifically to work in the Office of Smart Growth. For the Smart Growth office, this was an easy way to attract young, smart, and energetic recent college grads who, armed with master's degrees, were eager to work hard on cutting edge Smart Growth issues for two years at relatively low pay.

The OSG staff worked with developers, builders, and local governments on ways to improve the details of specific development projects; they developed educational and informational materials, speaker series,

**Fig. 11.3.** Governor Glendening (right) talks with newly appointed Office of Smart Growth Special Secretary Harriet Tregoning and Planning Secretary Roy Kienitz (second from left). Joining them are National Center for Smart Growth Research and Education Executive Director Tom Downs (third from left) and Office of Smart Growth Communications Director John W. Frece.

and other events about Smart Growth; and they developed guidelines for "best practices," such as a paper produced by Robin Zimbler, one of the office's bright young Policy Fellows, outlining strategies for improving parking requirements for Smart Growth developments.

Tregoning also convinced the governor to hire an old Washington pal of hers named Roy Kienitz to be her replacement at the Department of Planning. Kienitz had been chief of staff to U.S. Senator Daniel Patrick Moynihan of New York and later headed the Surface Transportation Policy Project, a Washington-based nonprofit organization that advocates for more balanced transportation systems. Kienitz's hiring brought to MDP someone thoroughly knowledgeable about transportation issues, especially federal transportation programs. While working for Moynihan, Kienitz had been largely responsible for drafting the federal transportation bill known as ISTEA[9] that broke open the sacrosanct federal highway fund for use on transit or other non-highway uses. The legislation also made the receipt of federal transportation funds by local governments contingent on conformance with the Clean Air Act.*

Even though the Maryland Department of Transportation under Secretary John D. Porcari was probably as progressive and pro–Smart Growth as any state transportation department this side of Oregon, the cultural change at the top of the department was slow in seeping down to the old guard engineers who were still doing much of the day-to-day work. It was hoped that Kienitz, with his deep understanding of federal transportation funding and alternative transportation concepts, could somehow influence MDOT from his perch at Planning.

The day Glendening announced Tregoning's transfer to the Office of Smart Growth, he also announced the hiring of Kienitz. Then the governor inadvertently buried the news of those two appointments by simultaneously announcing his intention to begin using a long dormant—and only recently discovered by Glendening's staff—authority to have the Department of Planning intervene in local planning decisions.† Once again, local

---

*Kienitz had also served on Glendening's Transportation Solutions Group and was one of four members who filed a minority report that strongly disagreed with the group's majority recommendation to build the ICC. "We strongly believe that the Intercounty Connector (ICC) has no place in this integrated approach, as it contradicts the very goals Maryland's Smart Growth Initiative and the Maryland Transportation Plan seek to achieve," the minority report stated. Source: "Providing More Travel Choices for Suburban Marylanders: Steps to Improve Mobility and Quality of Life in a Growing Region," Appendix B: Recommendations of the Minority Members of the Transportation Solutions Group, Report of the Transportation Solutions Group, July 15, 1999.

†This authority dated to the State Planning Act passed under Governor Marvin Mandel in 1974, but had rarely if ever been used.

governments shuddered at the thought of heavy-handed intervention by the state in local planning matters.

Kienitz became the administration's point person—and lightening rod—for the governor's new-found authority to intervene in local land use decisions. Glendening, nearing the end of his term and with less and less to lose politically, wanted to push it hard. But Kienitz instinctively understood how explosive this intervention authority could be, if mishandled.

Taking an extremely cautious approach designed to be strong enough to satisfy the governor, but deferential enough to mollify local officials, Kienitz embarked on a strategy of "intervening"—at least at first—only in cases in which the state could side with local governments. The Department of Planning dispatched lawyers, for example, to help the city of Chestertown, which was still fighting the same Wal-Mart proposal that had caught Glendening's attention some five years earlier. It sided with the city of Annapolis—and against local NIMBYs—in support of a moderate density development on the downtown site of a recently demolished hospital.

In time, Kienitz and his staff grew bolder. When the Carroll County Commission voted to rezone agricultural land to permit more development in rural areas, for instance, Kienitz fired a shot across the county's bow. If they did not reconsider and reverse their action, he warned, the state would have no choice but to deny the county funds for farmland preservation. The threat worked and the county reversed itself.

Frece, meanwhile, as communications director of the new Office of Smart Growth, set about drafting and revising new Smart Growth publications, establishing an Office of Smart Growth Web page, setting up a Smart Growth speakers' series, staging a student Smart Growth art contest, helping create a series of Smart Growth lesson plans for use by high school teachers, and putting on annual, day-long Governor's Youth Environmental Summits that brought together hundreds of high school students and their teachers to discuss and debate Smart Growth issues. The highlight of the day was always a session in which the students could directly ask questions of the governor of Maryland.

## Scoring Smart Growth Projects

Tregoning rounded out the staff by hiring three policy and planning specialists, Suzanne Cartwright, Julia Koster, and Sam Bradner, to comprise OSG's "projects team." The team was to work directly with developers, local governments, or other state agencies on specific development projects to assure that, to the extent possible, they conformed to Smart Growth principles and goals.

Koster, the first of the three to be hired, was immediately assigned the task of developing a "Smart Growth Scorecard." As the Smart Growth program—and the governor's personal interest in it—had become

**Fig. 11.4.** Maryland's gubernatorial level Office of Smart Growth opened for business in summer 2001. The staff during the office's heyday included: (front row, left to right) Suzanne Cartwright, Sandra Olek, Christine Shenot, Harriet Tregoning, Arabia Matthews, and Barbara Wells; (back row, left to right) Michael Li, Robin Zimbler, John Frece, Jessica Cogan, Sam Bradner, Danielle Glaros, Marty Guinane, Mary Matheny, and Julia Koster.

increasingly well known, more and more developers began labeling their projects as "Smart Growth projects." Whether this was done to curry favor with the governor, to attract project funding from the state, or simply to market the projects to a public sympathetic to Smart Growth goals was never certain. What was certain was that the label "Smart Growth" was being co-opted. Many of the projects that claimed to be "Smart Growth" projects were often located far from any existing communities, or failed to offer housing for different income levels, or open space and walkways, or mixes of uses or transit connections. One OSG staffer recalled being invited to speak about Smart Growth to a conference of highway contractors and was surprised to see an item on the agenda entitled, "Building Tomorrow's Smart Growth Highways."

Increasingly, developers were turning to the state—to the Maryland Department of Planning, or to the governor's assistant for Smart Growth or, later, to the Office of Smart Growth—for a Smart Growth seal of approval. Such recognition was suddenly seen as something of value. It might represent the last push a project needed to get it past a local planning commission or a reluctant county council. But Tregoning realized the state had no objective way to judge which projects were genuinely Smart Growth projects and which were not.

Koster, a young planner from Washington state, spent her first months in the Office of Smart Growth reviewing scorecards or similar instruments used in other jurisdictions around the country to rate or rank projects. She pieced together drafts that she thought might work in Maryland and field-tested them with builders, developers, and other planners. The scorecard's first question was its most important: Where is the project located? It went on to measure the mix of uses, the mix of housing types, the adjacency to transit (if appropriate), and the potential "walkability" of the community, among other tests. Before long, developers were calling the Office of Smart Growth to ask if they could share their plans with the projects team and get their feedback. In some instances, there was clearly an interest in obtaining a letter from OSG saying that a certain project scored high on the Smart Growth scorecard.

One advantage the projects team had was that its work was non-threatening. The OSG had no authority to force changes in plans; it could only recommend changes or point out shortcomings. As a result, developers and others clamored for assistance, often showing up at OSG's door in Annapolis with rolls of blueprints tucked under their arms.

The staff intentionally shied away from using numerical scores or grades, but rather used the scorecard to show the general range of compliance with Smart Growth expectations. In some cases, subsequent support by the Office of Smart Growth tipped the balance in favor of some projects, but in other cases it was still not enough to persuade skeptical local officials to vote "Aye."

In time, Frece decided Glendening had been right about the Office
of Smart Growth after all. Glendening always believed that one cabinet
secretary, such as the secretary of Planning, could not tell other cabinet
secretaries what to do. But he felt the special secretary for Smart Growth
could do so because of the proximity to and implied authority from the
governor himself. Tregoning seemed to prove that theory to be correct.

More importantly, it became clear the Office of Smart Growth was the
only agency in government looking at the "big picture"—the only agency
whose job was to look at the performance of multiple agencies toward the
achievement of a set of general goals. It was the one agency with that could
speak on behalf of the governor to force one recalcitrant department to
work with another. Smart Growth had given all the different agencies a
role in implementation, but until the Office of Smart Growth was established, there was no comprehensive effort to coordinate these activities.

# Chapter 12

# A Conservative's Opportunity

Parris Glendening was proud to be a liberal, although in public he preferred to call himself a "progressive" for fear the liberal tag might somehow hurt him. But Glendening always thought Smart Growth was a fundamentally conservative approach to governance and never ceased to marvel at that irony.

Smart Growth sought to conserve natural resources from wasteful development patterns, to save land, to maximize government infrastructure investments in older communities, and to protect taxpayers from the high cost of building new and often redundant infrastructure to support new development. Glendening thought conservatives should embrace all of these goals.

A policy wonk at heart, Glendening understood the efficiencies that could be gained by curtailing long-distance commuting as a strategy to reduce air pollution and transportation project costs. He knew that if the state could somehow contain sprawl development, the amount of new impervious surface that is created would also decline, reducing the nutrient and pollution runoff that is so harmful to the Chesapeake Bay and its tributaries and so costly to remediate once it is in the water.

Glendening, who in his first term became so reviled by business organizations that they sued him over the issue of collective bargaining, liked to tell business groups that "Smart Growth is smart for business." He was absolutely convinced there was a ready market for well-designed, higher density, mixed use, walkable communities such as Kentlands in Montgomery County. Builders and others in the business community, he believed, would be financially well served if they embraced Smart Growth. He was certain the public would pay a premium for centrally located, well-designed housing that was close to transit, close to stores, and close to cultural activities.

The conservative nature of the Smart Growth initiative, he thought, actually contributed to its broad and often bipartisan appeal. He proudly talked about how he saw eye to eye with Republican governors such as Christie Todd Whitman of New Jersey or Mike Leavitt of Utah, both of whom were pushing Smart Growth programs in their own states.*

Glendening had every reason to believe Smart Growth was a program that was here to stay. He had institutionalized it in several Maryland statutes, by gubernatorial executive order, and by changing the way state agencies did business. By using the "bully pulpit" of his office, he had forced local governments to pay attention to growth issues and made the issue of growth a regular topic in the political dialogue of the state. The phrase "Smart Growth" slipped into the vocabulary of the public and the news media alike, as did the concept behind the two words. Smart Growth became a national issue, the focus of huge annual national conferences, and Maryland was often invited to be the guest of honor at these events.

When the National Wildlife Federation opened a new headquarters on a large campus reachable only by car in the Fairfax County suburb of Reston, Va., the *Washington Post* wrote an article accusing the nonprofit organization of hypocrisy: promoting Smart Growth on the one hand, but locating its headquarters in a sprawl-like setting. If Maryland had not made "Smart Growth" a household concept by then, it is fair to suggest that the *Post* would never have seen the Wildlife Federation's location decision as a news story.[1]

More comforting for Smart Growth supporters, there was every reason to believe the next governor of Maryland would continue and perhaps expand the program. After all, every Maryland governor since Marvin Mandel—a span of more than thirty years—had pushed for a gradual strengthening of the state's land use and environmental protection laws. It was not that they did the same thing, but that they and the General Assembly steadily pushed the state in essentially the same direction.

Glendening's lieutenant governor was Kathleen Kennedy Townsend, daughter of Robert F. Kennedy, niece of President John F. Kennedy, and Glendening's heir apparent. Townsend had worked just across the second floor of the State House from Glendening for eight years, but neither she nor her staff had ever been involved in his Smart Growth efforts. Her portfolio primarily involved law and order issues. Yet Townsend was sympathetic and supportive, saying during her campaign for governor that she intended to continue the Smart Growth program and to retain Tregoning to run it. Frece was periodically invited to serve as her staff at

---

*Governors Whitman and Leavitt would later become President George W. Bush's first and second administrators of the U.S. Environmental Protection Agency, where both supported the continuation of the EPA's Smart Growth work originally started in the office once headed by Harriet Tregoning.

**Fig. 12.1.** Lt. Gov. Kathleen Kennedy Townsend (left) was widely expected to succeed Gov. Parris Glendening, but lost the 2002 election to Republican Robert L. Ehrlich, Jr. Photo courtesy of the *Baltimore Sun*.

events at which she discussed growth, transportation, or related issues with homebuilders, environmentalists, and others.

Townsend was considered such a shoo-in to become Glendening's successor that several other potential candidates decided against challenging her in the 2002 Democratic Primary. She had name recognition, the power of incumbency, and an ability to raise campaign money. She was running in a heavily Democratic state and the road ahead looked clear.

## A Conservative Takes Over

It was all a sure thing—until she lost. The upset winner was Robert L. Ehrlich Jr., a congressman from Baltimore County and former state delegate, who became the first Republican elected governor of Maryland since Spiro T. Agnew in 1966. Ehrlich was a blue-collar kid who had parlayed talent on the football field into a scholarship to an elite private school in Baltimore and a college education at Princeton. He became a lawyer, a state legislator and member of the House Judiciary Committee, and then a congressman during the heyday of House Speaker Newt Gingrich's Republican revolution. Despite these credentials, he was expected to be the Republican's sacrificial lamb in the 2002 gubernatorial race. But the public had tired of Glendening and the Democrats, never warmed to Townsend, and elected Ehrlich, who ran a far better campaign. Townsend's votes came from Baltimore and the state's other urbanized areas; Ehrlich won big in the suburbs.

When Bob Ehrlich arrived back in Annapolis in January 2003, neither he nor his small group of loyal staff really knew what they wanted to do with state government. After all, they hadn't expected to win. There was seemingly no end to the questions or issues they had to address: cabinet appointments, budget decisions, the hiring of staff, figuring out positions on issues, relations with the legislature, and putting on an inauguration. The biggest problem facing the new governor was a huge budget deficit that was the product of Glendening's final year of robust spending, an expensive new school aid program the General Assembly enacted in an election year without benefit of enough revenue to cover its cost, and a sharp national recession. Maryland's Constitution requires a balanced budget, so unlike in the Congress he had just left, Ehrlich had to figure out how to keep his expenditures in line with his revenues. And, like so many Republicans around the nation, Ehrlich had campaigned on a promise not to raise taxes.

The new governor's answer to all of this was to propose the legalization of slot machine gambling. Slots had once been legal in four Southern Maryland counties, but were outlawed in 1968, and repeated attempts to bring them back had been blocked. The governor's proposal was so controversial that it diverted attention from almost everything else in his

**Fig. 12.2.** Gov. Robert L. Ehrlich, Jr. (right) found an ally in Comptroller (and former Governor) William Donald Schaefer (left). Photo courtesy of the *Baltimore Sun.*

first General Assembly session until his slots legislation finally died in a House committee.*

While all of this was going on, the few remaining souls in the depleted Office of Smart Growth were trying their best to interest the new governor in keeping the Smart Growth initiative moving forward. Kienitz had been asked to leave at Planning; Tregoning had resigned. Cartwright left for a job in Washington and Cogan concluded she couldn't work for a Republican administration. Frece, Koster, Bradner, and young Dannielle Glaros, Cogan's deputy, were left to run the office with Frece serving as director.

Frece had known Ehrlich from the time he was a first-term state legislator and Frece was a *Baltimore Sun* reporter covering the State House. They had once been on a first-name basis. Frece also had been friends with Ehrlich's communications director, Paul Schurick, from the days when Schurick worked for Governor William Donald Schaefer. There seemed to be a reasonable chance to get the new governor's ear and that the Smart Growth program could be continued, but refocused to meet the political needs of the new Republican administration.

After all, Smart Growth was not regulatory. It was an incentive-based program in which many of the financial incentives ultimately went to the same development community that generally made up the core of the Republican Party's campaign base. And, as Glendening was fond of pointing out, it was a fundamentally conservative approach that ought to appeal to the conservative Republicans who were moving into the State House.

Here was an opportunity for a conservative Republican to remake the Smart Growth program to fit his own conservative philosophy and goals. Ehrlich may have been elected, but Democrats still controlled both houses of the legislature and outnumbered Republicans two to one in voter registration. It seemed that should be incentive enough—the challenge of getting anything through a potentially hostile legislature and the need, then still four years away, to appeal to Democrats in a reelection campaign—for the new governor to pursue a moderate or middle-of-the-road political course. A program such as Smart Growth seemed to be a ready-made way for Ehrlich to acquire some quick environmental credentials. Smart Growth was popular with legislators and generally popular with the public. Why not latch onto a good thing and repackage it?

The reduced Office of Smart Growth staff set about the task of preparing and sending to the governor's State House staff a series of memos outlining how the program could be reshaped to fit a GOP agenda and continued. A four-page memo submitted in February 2003 listed eight separate activities in which the Office of Smart Growth could help the new

---

*Ehrlich tried to enact slots legislation again in his second and third legislative sessions in 2004 and 2005, again without success.

administration—everything from working on specific, ongoing projects to events that could raise the new governor's profile on Smart Growth issues.

Some of the ideas were complicated and difficult, such as working with the departments of transportation and environment to implement a new "Smart Growth State Implementation Plan" through which Smart Growth development would be used to help meet federal air quality mitigation requirements. Others were more directly attuned to the governor's own priorities, such as proposing intense revitalization efforts in the neighborhoods adjacent to the state's horse racing tracks, where Ehrlich hoped to legalize slot machines.[2]

Many of Ehrlich's staff, however, had come with him from Capitol Hill and appeared to have little interest in finding ways to work on the major program of Ehrlich's Democratic predecessor. No response came from the memos suggesting how the Smart Growth program might be reframed. Rather, the governor's staff reacted to Smart Growth with skepticism. Despite an extensive briefing to Ehrlich's transition team, almost no one on the governor's staff seemed to understand what Smart Growth was all about or see how they might use it to their own advantage.

Unlike Glendening and many of his aides, Ehrlich and most members of his new State House staff had never worked in local government and therefore never had reason to deal with development proposals, zoning, or land use decisions. His aides seemed to suspect Smart Growth was nothing more than a program designed to promote Glendening politically—pure politics and no substance.

Ehrlich appointed Audrey E. Scott, a former three-term mayor of Bowie and later the lone Republican on the Prince George's County Council, to replace Kienitz as secretary of planning. For a decade during the administrations of presidents Ronald Reagan and George H. W. Bush, Scott worked in the U.S. Department of Housing and Urban Development, first as special assistant in community planning and development and later as general deputy assistant secretary. But Scott, too, was suspicious of the Office of Smart Growth, viewing it as a competitor to her new agency, the Maryland Department of Planning. MDP, she thought, was the department that rightfully should be leading whatever Smart Growth efforts the new administration might push. She said she had been told that staff at MDP did most of the work while staff at the Office of Smart Growth got most of the glory and implied that was about to change.

In the twelve weeks immediately following Ehrlich's January 2003 inauguration, however, there was little time for Scott or others on the governor's staff to make solid judgments about anything, including what to do about the Smart Growth program in general or the Office of Smart Growth in particular. They were too immersed in their first legislative session. For lack of any other strategy, Ehrlich's chief of staff instructed the

OSG staff to lobby the legislature to keep the office and its budget intact. That, at least, would preserve the status quo until the legislature ended in April and Ehrlich and his staff would have time to decide about the future of Smart Growth.

Backed by Ehrlich aide and former state senator Martin D. Madden, Frece testified before budget committees in both houses, explaining what he saw as the significance of the new office and why it should be continued.

"The Governor's Office of Smart Growth is unique because it is the only unit of state government responsible for trying to make sure there is an overall Smart Growth outcome in all that we do. It is the one office that is charged with the task of looking out for the 'big picture' and trying to assure that what the state is doing in land use is sustainable over the long run," he testified.[3]

"The Office of Smart Growth does not bring direct funding to a project, but rather relies on the considerable skills and resources of other agencies. What we do is the tough job of being a neutral coordinator between agencies by keeping the focus on a Smart Growth outcome. That, in turn, creates efficiency in applying state resources, allows each agency to focus on doing its job effectively, and creates the critical mass of effort that is so often needed to get a project going."[4]

The OSG director noted that several other states, including New Jersey, Massachusetts, Michigan, and Maine, were considering establishing units of government modeled after Maryland's Office of Smart Growth.

"There is probably no other policy of state government that encompasses such a wide and seemingly disparate set of issues as Smart Growth," Frece said. "The governor's Office of Smart Growth occupies a unique position within state government that allows it to provide the unique service of overseeing such a broad concept. It represents the most effective way to implement the General Assembly's strong and consistent commitment to Smart Growth because it is the only entity in state government that is trying to keep tabs on the state's overall Smart Growth results."[5]

Despite recommendations from legislative analysts to cut the budget and core staff of the Office of Smart Growth and merge the remainder with the Department of Planning, the General Assembly did none of that. It approved the Office of Smart Growth budget in full.

The OSG staff also helped the new administration stave off an assault by the General Assembly on the state's historic preservation tax credit program. The program had become one of the state's most effective redevelopment tools. A study released a year before Ehrlich's first legislative session concluded that "historic preservation and related tax credits result not only in the upgrading of historic buildings in Maryland, but also increased jobs and resident incomes. The state and local jurisdictions benefit from increased tax revenues. The Maryland economy benefits and the increased tax revenues offset much of the historic tax credit. In addition, the state's investment leverages private investment dollars and federal historic tax credits." Moreover, the report said, "[t]he economic and fiscal activity attributable to historic rehabilitation occurs before the state pays out its historic tax credits."[6]

But some legislators said they worried the tax break was becoming too costly to the state, that developers were enriching themselves at tax-payers' expense, and that too many of the projects were in a single juris-diction, Baltimore. In the 2000–2001 study year, more than half of the tax credits for commercial projects and nearly a quarter of all residential projects had gone to Baltimore. But, as the study indicated, "[g]iven the age of the city's building stock . . . [and the] many historic neighbor-hoods and buildings in need of physical repair and renovation," that re-sult was neither surprising nor bad.[7] It only slowly dawned on legislators that the revenue from the historic preservation projects almost always ex-ceeded the cost of the tax credit, that without providing benefits to de-velopers they would never embark on some of these risky redevelopment projects, and that Baltimore was the city that probably needed the most redevelopment help.

Once Ehrlich's first legislative session was over, however, the OSG telephones went silent. Calls and memos to the governor's staff went unanswered. A staff-to-staff meeting with Scott quickly developed an ugly edge, with the new secretary making clear that she—not the Office of Smart Growth—would decide when and whether to summon the Smart Growth Sub-Cabinet to meet or to take other action related to the Smart Growth program. Ehrlich administration appointees began moving into empty offices at the Office of Smart Growth and interviewing OSG staff about the OSG budget.

By June, all but four members of the original OSG staff had either left voluntarily or were fired, and the four were transferred to a low-level unit within MDP. The Office of Smart Growth still existed in state statute, but every position there had been emptied and its Annapolis offices turned over to other agencies.

Appearing before county planners at the annual meeting of the Maryland Association of Counties in Ocean City that summer, Scott pub-licly asserted that everyone who had left the Office of Smart Growth had done so of their own free will and that those who had been moved to MDP "think they have died and gone to heaven."[8]

Despite such public pronouncements, the political momentum for Smart Growth, which had been building steadily for seven years, had stopped. For months afterward, state employees who had been involved in the Smart Growth effort during the Glendening years confessed pri-vately that they were afraid even to utter the phrase "Smart Growth" aloud or admit they had ever worked with the Office of Smart Growth. The new administration was purging state agencies of employees that were too closely identified with Glendening or the Democratic Party and many feared for their jobs.

## Priority Places

By fall, however, the paranoia began to dissipate and some mid-level staff at MDP began to make modest efforts to get the Smart Growth program off life support and moving again. Internally, they had spent part of the summer struggling with what to call the initiative. Should they stick with the name "Smart Growth" so identified with Glendening, or come up with something new? In the end, they decided to do both, putting the new governor's own stamp on the program while conceding that the brand name "Smart Growth" was too well known to ignore.

In October 2003, Ehrlich issued an executive order that announced the creation of his own Smart Growth program, which he called "Priority Places."[9] The executive order reaffirmed the value of sound land use policy and explained that the new "Priority Places strategy" was part of the state's broader Smart Growth effort. The executive order put the Maryland Department of Planning in charge.

That same month, Ehrlich also hosted the ninth annual Smart Growth Awards. Again, the new administration changed the name of the event, calling it the "Vision Awards." In its press release announcing the newly named Vision Awards, MDP explained that the awards would "recognize outstanding work in Smart Growth."

The concept of Priority Places was to identify relatively small, specific neighborhoods that would become a "priority place" for the state to target its resources. The strategy was similar to the "Designated Neighborhood" program that had been employed by the Department of Housing and Community Development during the Glendening administration and which had funneled state funds to neighborhoods for revitalization. The difference between the two programs, however, was key: "Designated Neighborhoods" offered local governments money; Priority Places did not. In lieu of money, the Ehrlich administration promised to expedite projects, although most permitting requirements that tended to slow projects resided at the local level, not the state.

After four years, only seven communities in the entire state were designated as Priority Places. Without the prospect of receiving money, the number of applicants fell from twenty-two to fourteen to nine, prompting Douglas Burkhardt, who became the director of MDP's Office of Smart Growth in 2006, to say: "I think people have wised up to what the value of Priority Places is."[10]

## Measuring Development Capacity

For several years before Ehrlich was elected, Maryland home builders had been complaining about the shrinking availability of raw land for development. The home builders variously blamed environmental restrictions, Smart Growth laws, or local project opponents for their plight. Whatever the cause, the home builders were convinced they were running out of land on which to build. As proof positive, they pointed to the rising cost of housing in Maryland and the fundamental laws of supply and demand. But Maryland's counties, they discovered, either did not have the data to show how much land they had available for new development or refused to calculate the amount.

The home builders, led primarily by their Baltimore regional chapter, the Home Builders Association of Maryland, commissioned studies to prove their point and began to lobby the General Assembly to require counties to conduct "land lot inventories."[11] The Priority Funding Areas legislation enacted in 1997 directed counties to conduct "an analysis of the capacity of land areas available for development, including infill and redevelopment; and, an analysis of the land area needed to satisfy demand for development at densities consistent with the Master Plan."[12] But as the individual county PFA maps began to trickle into the Maryland Department of Planning for review, it became obvious that some counties were doing a far better job than others in estimating future capacity. Some did not appear to be doing it at all.

In September 2001, the Smart Growth citizen advocacy organization, 1000 Friends of Maryland, published a study[13] rating the Smart Growth performance of five counties in the metropolitan Baltimore region. "We were astonished to learn how inadequate and incomplete the information necessary to evaluate county policies was," the report stated. "Counties, municipalities, the Baltimore Metropolitan Council, and state agencies all lacked basic and essential information about where construction is taking place, how many miles of roads they plan on constructing and what our neighborhoods look like. Jurisdictions routinely used estimates and other substitutes for quantitative information."

Counties, however, fought the idea of being required to perform the land lot inventories, saying they didn't have the staff, time or money to do it and criticized the proposal as "an unfunded mandate." The Ehrlich administration, which had received strong campaign support from home builders, had a more sympathetic ear than the Democratic-controlled legislature.

In November 2003, the new governor appointed a nine-member Development Capacity Task Force to do pilot studies in five counties and five municipalities for the purpose of developing a standard protocol for estimating future development capacity. Chaired by Secretary Scott, the task force also included representatives of municipal and county governments, home builders, environmentalists, historic preservationists, economic development officials, and the director of the National Center for Smart Growth Research and Education at the University of Maryland.

The task force met regularly for eight months and concluded its work by signing a Memorandum of Understanding between the state and the Maryland Association of Counties (representing the state's twenty-three counties) and the Maryland Municipal League (representing Maryland's 156 incorporated municipalities). The MOU stipulated the standard method that local jurisdictions would use in estimating future development capacity.

On August 19, 2004, Governor Ehrlich issued a second executive order[14] that extended the life of the task force until August 2008 and directed the Department of Planning to provide local governments with technical assistance needed to properly estimate future development capacity. It also directed MDP to consult with the Development Capacity Task Force to develop a schedule for local jurisdictions to conduct their capacity analyses and required MDP to review local comprehensive plans to assure that development capacity analyses are included pursuant to the procedures outlined in the MOU.[15]

At their last few meetings, members of the task force hotly debated whether the local governments should be required to perform the development capacity analysis or merely encouraged to do so—what some described as the question of "should versus shall." In the end the task force opted for the less regulatory approach favored by the local jurisdictions. Nonetheless, in his executive order extending the task force's life, the governor directed task force members to decide after two years whether local governments are conducting the capacity analyses as agreed to in the MOU and, if not, whether "legislative remedies" may be necessary to assure that these analyses are conducted.

## Smart Growth Under Attack

Despite the progress made in pushing local governments to do a better job estimating future development capacity, other elements of Maryland's Smart Growth initiative steadily atrophied. A program based on the concept of offering incentives as a means of prompting changes in development decisions found itself with few incentives to offer. The new governor no longer used the bully pulpit of his office to chide local governments into adhering to Smart Growth goals, instead espousing a hands-off policy toward local land use decisions. By the second year of the Ehrlich administration, the Smart Growth program was under attack on almost all fronts.

Much of the Smart Growth brain trust had voluntarily left or had been pushed out of state government: Kreitner, Young, and Kienitz were gone from Planning; Tregoning, Cogan, Frece, Cartwright, Glaros, and Koster from the Office of Smart Growth; revitalization specialist Ellen Janes and historic preservation specialist Bill Pencek from Housing and Community Development; Transportation Secretary John Porcari, State

Highway Administrator Parker Williams, and long-range transit planner Henry Kay were all gone; Lauren Wenzel, who had worked with Tributary Teams and on Smart Growth education for the Department of Natural Resources, environmental speechwriter Tom Burke, land preservation administrator Grant Dehart, and environmental specialist David Burke, who developed DNR's landmark GreenPrint lands inventory, were all gone. So were Assistant Secretary Verna Harrison and much of her staff, which had worked together for years on Chesapeake Bay protection measures. A core group of planners within the Department of Planning with years of experience on Smart Growth issues remained, but they were submerged by an entirely new layer of assistant secretaries brought into the department by Ehrlich and Scott.

By January 2004, the administration had also decided what it wanted to do about the Office of Smart Growth: abolish it.[16] The office had already been emptied of personnel so abolition would have had no practical effect. But the Democrats who controlled the General Assembly viewed repeal as a symbolic stake in the heart of Smart Growth and rejected it.

"I think there's some important symbolism," observed Stewart Schwartz, executive director of the Coalition for Smarter Growth, a Washington-area advocacy group. "It downgrades the role of Smart Growth in the state."[17]

The more serious damage was inflicted on various incentive programs offered under the Smart Growth banner. Facing a deficit, refusing to raise taxes, and unable to get slot machines legalized, the Ehrlich administration had no choice but to cut existing programs.

The Live Near Your Work housing assistance program was zeroed out in the budget,* as was the Department of Transportation's popular Neighborhood Conservation initiative. Revenues from a real estate transfer tax that by law were to be dedicated to Program Open Space, the state's parkland acquisition program, instead were siphoned off to help balance the general state budget. The Community Parks and Playgrounds program, designed to improve and expand parks in urbanized areas as a strategy to make higher density living more acceptable, was zeroed out in Ehrlich's first year. It would have been zeroed out his second year as well had the legislature not insisted on restoring it.

Other land preservation programs, which had peaked under Glendening, were cut so sharply that most land preservation activity in the state staggered to a halt. During Glendening's eight years in office, an array of state and local land preservation programs were employed together to save more than 285,000 acres, or nearly 4 percent of the land

_____

*This small but popular program was resurrected by Ehrlich in 2006, but as a loan rather than grant program. More troubling to Smart Growth proponents, the revised Live Near Your Work program defined living near your work as anywhere within a radius of twenty-five miles.

mass of the state. That nearly matched the 325,000 acres that had been protected by all of the governors together who preceded Glendening from 1970, when the state began protecting land under Program Open Space. With Glendening's funding support and new initiatives, the state was able to protect more land than was developed every year except one between Fiscal Year 1997 and Fiscal Year 2003.

In Glendening's most ambitious year, fiscal year 2002, the state spent nearly $56 million to buy land and development rights under just two of the state's land preservation programs, Rural Legacy and GreenPrint. In Ehrlich's first budget in FY 2004, that number plummeted to $10 million and the following year fell again to $5 million—barely enough at current land prices in Maryland to buy one large farm.

The Ehrlich administration also came to office with a different attitude toward transportation, supporting highway projects the Glendening administration had resisted and deemphasizing transit projects Glendening had championed. Glendening and his transportation secretary, John D. Porcari, tried to get more balance in the state's overall transportation system. But Ehrlich's new transportation secretary, former Howard County State Delegate Robert Flanagan, turned the highway builders loose, embarking on several high profile, controversial, and extremely expensive highway projects.

The biggest was the Intercounty Connector, the long-proposed, east-west highway across Montgomery County linking the I-270 corridor with the I-95 corridor north of the Capital Beltway. Glendening had been an ICC supporter when he was first elected, but changed his tune in later years, saying he opposed the road because of the environmental damage it would cause and because, at the time, local governments also opposed it. His Transportation Solutions Group, which studied the corridor and reported its findings to Glendening after his 1998 reelection was over, recommended a highway be built in the corridor, but said access should be limited, tolls should be charged that increase with the level of congestion, and trucks prohibited. Importantly, the group failed to identify a preferred alignment.

Porcari, Glendening's transportation secretary, said he tried to get the federally required environmental impact statement completed so the decision could be decided on its merits, but Glendening "made up his mind [to halt the project] and there was no discussing it with him."[18] At one point, Glendening even tried to authorize the sale of parcels of rights-of-way purchased along the proposed ICC alignment, but he was blocked from doing so by the other two members of the Board of Public Works. Washington area business leaders who had supported Glendening's initial candidacy in 1994 partly because of his support for the ICC felt betrayed.

During the 2002 campaign, however, both Ehrlich and Townsend said they would build the ICC, if elected. Congestion had become such a serious problem in the Washington suburbs that neither felt they could win without supporting the ICC. It was such a potent political issue it almost didn't matter if the official studies showed the road would likely have little impact on Capital Beltway congestion.

"I met separately with Kathleen on this and she was my ally to finish the study," recalled Porcari. "We had a meeting in [Room] 217 and she argued passionately to build the ICC. I remember vividly Parris saying to her, 'You're going to have to disagree with me on some things, but not now, not on this one.'"[19] Porcari said he believes Townsend hurt her own election chances by failing to separate herself earlier from Glendening and coming out publicly in support of the ICC earlier than she did. "Parris basically cut her legs off by saying, 'You can't publicly dissent on this.'"

The other controversial road pushed by the Ehrlich administration was the widening of Route 32 in rural Howard County, Flanagan's home county. Plans to make the two-lane road into a dual lane road were slowed during the Glendening administration because of fear the wider, faster road would only encourage more sprawl development in a still fairly pastoral section of Howard County. After the Ehrlich administration announced plans to move forward with the project, it was promptly sued by 1000 Friends of Maryland in an attempt to stop the construction. The suit ultimately failed and the project is still being planned.

## The Purple Line

Glendening had also tried to put in motion plans to build the first phase of a circumferential transit line around the city of Washington. Called the "Purple Line," it would have connected the ends of the spokes of the Metro subway system that radiated out from the center of the city to various suburban termination points. To get from one suburban station to another, a rider now must take a train into the city and back out again, a lengthy and time-consuming trip that few riders are willing to make. Instead, they usually drive their cars. This connection, which would be built essentially parallel to the Capital Beltway, had become increasingly important as jobs and housing moved out from the city to the surrounding suburbs in Maryland and Virginia.

Again, cost became the critical factor for the new administration. With virtually all of its transportation revenues earmarked for the $2 billion to $3 billion ICC project, there was little money and less political will left to support the Purple Line, too. Instead, the Department of Transportation returned to the drawing board to investigate the idea of running a dedicated busway rather than tracks along the Purple Line alignment. At the end of four years, neither a bus nor rail line was in place along the Purple Line alignment.

While the new highway-oriented leadership at the Department of Transportation seemed increasingly cool toward transit, their staff nevertheless continued to work on transit-oriented-development ("TOD") projects near existing Metro stops in or near Hyattsville, Silver Spring, New Carrollton, and Rockville.[20]

## The "Flush Tax"

Governor Ehrlich's most highly touted environmental achievement was a $2.50 fee per household per month imposed in 2004 on all sewer and septic customers as well as a flow-based fee imposed on industry. Proceeds from what was dubbed "the Flush Tax" created a Chesapeake Bay Restoration Fund that was to provide the money needed to improve nutrient removal at sewage treatment facilities as well as provide funds to help farmers curtail harmful agricultural runoff. But from a Smart Growth perspective, even this environmental achievement turned sour when it came to light that wastewater treatment plant improvements were being used to justify more sprawl development.[21]

"This is at best a missed opportunity and likely a real significant blow to state Smart Growth policies," said J. Charles Fox, a U.S. Environmental Protection Agency official who had been Secretary of Natural Resources in Glendening's final year.[22]

In March 2005, the nonprofit Maryland League of Conservation Voters published a "Gubernatorial Mid-Term Report Card" in which the Ehrlich administration was graded on eight separate environmental issues.[23] His overall grade was a D+. In 2006, the League lowered Ehrlich's grade to D and endorsed his opponent in the 2006 gubernatorial election, Baltimore Mayor Martin O'Malley.

"Maryland's natural resources and the health and quality of life of its citizens are threatened by rapid, poorly planned development," LCV's 2005 report stated in its Smart Growth section. "While Governor Ehrlich showed some promise in preserving historic preservation tax credits and supporting brownfields cleanup and redevelopment efforts, his dismantling of the successful Office of Smart Growth and the proposed widening of Route 32 has set the state back years in its work to preserve Maryland lands while planning for sensible growth."[24]

The 2005 report in particular was stingingly critical of an attempt by the Ehrlich administration to resell eight hundred acres of forest land in St. Mary's County to a politically connected commercial developer. Soon, reports surfaced that the administration had developed a list of other protected lands it was considering declaring as "excess" and selling. Glendening had made his name, in part, through aggressive land protection efforts; Ehrlich appeared headed in the opposite direction.

The public furor that resulted over the proposed land sales prompted the General Assembly to propose a constitutional amendment that would prohibit any governor from selling off lands owned and protected by the

**Fig. 12.3.** Baltimore Mayor Martin O'Malley (right), shown here with Glendening, defeated Ehrlich for governor in 2006. Photo courtesy of the *Baltimore Sun*.

state without prior General Assembly approval. Ehrlich initially opposed the legislation, saying it would tie his hands, but once he and his staff recognized how broad the public support for it was, they capitulated and the governor announced he would back the bill. The public overwhelmingly voted to approve the measure in November 2006.*

The public also chose O'Malley to replace Ehrlich as governor, making Ehrlich the only incumbent governor in the nation to lose his reelection bid in 2006. Neither Smart Growth nor environmental issues were major focuses of their bitter campaign, although O'Malley tried to distinguish himself from the incumbent on both issues.

The Baltimore mayor, for example, criticized Ehrlich for deemphasizing Smart Growth and pledged to restart the stalled program, if elected. Although he provided few details about what that might mean, he made several general campaign promises:

- To set a goal of preserving more land each year than is consumed by development;
- To fully fund each year the state's parkland acquisition program, Program Open Space;
- To reestablish the Office of Smart Growth "with a new emphasis on creating a genuine partnership with municipalities and counties on how best to plan for and manage the growth that is coming to Maryland, and bring a stronger focus to encouraging growth in older communities—where we have infrastructure and public support for redevelopment";
- To increase technical and financial assistance to local governments to help them plan for growth; and,
- To invest in transit and telecommuting.[25]

He also began to restore Smart Growth supporters to key positions in government. He brought back John D. Porcari to again head the Department of Transportation and returned John R. Griffin to rebuild the Department of Natural Resources. He named Shari T. Wilson, a lawyer and brownfields expert who had briefly worked with the Office of Smart Growth and had been the Department of Environment's liaison on Smart Growth issues before leaving state service during the Ehrlich years, to head her old Department of Environment. And, he chose Richard Eberhardt Hall, a career planner and Smart Growth proponent within MDP who also headed the Maryland chapter of the American Planning Association, to be the Planning department's new secretary.

---

*The measure was approved, 1,361,956 to 241,188, and was approved in all twenty-four jurisdictions in the state.

# Chapter 13

## Political Lessons from the Maryland Experiment

Sound planning is important, but a sound political approach is just as important. A plan without an accompanying political strategy is probably a plan that will never be implemented.

Land use change requires a long incubation period. A major development project can take five to ten years to move from inception through zoning and subdivision approval, environmental permitting, approval for utilities, and a waiting period to assure compliance with local adequate public facilities ordinances. With growing frequency, projects that obtain required approvals are appealed by local opponents, adding months and often years to the process. A highway project can stay on the books for forty years without the first shovel of dirt being turned and take five to ten years or more to build once all approvals are granted. Transit planners routinely think in thirty- to fifty-year time horizons.

Change in land use plans is also gradual. Plans are developed, zoning approved, regulations drafted, and then all are changed and updated piecemeal over time. With changing leadership, institutional memory is often lost, giving way to a constant sense of "starting over" as if nothing came before. Such changes are prompted by varied and often simultaneous forces: demographic shifts in the population; the actions of one jurisdiction that have unintentional effects on neighboring jurisdictions; the advent of trendy new views in city planning or architectural design; or the often harsh economic realities of the building industry, governmental finances, or the cost of living of the citizenry.

Such change is inescapably intertwined with politics: the influence of a powerful or dynamic political leader who demands change, or the neglect by one who could care less about the issue. These issues are affected by either the interventionist or the hands-off philosophy of

elected officials; by the constant political struggle over who should have
the power of decision making; by the often hidden but clearly influential
effect on the political process of campaign contributions from the building and development industry; by the meshing of raw political ambition
with substantive policy debate; and by the ability—or inability—of government leaders to communicate a vision or a position that resonates
with the public.

In the realm of land use policy, who is to say when or what has to
happen before a specific city or town or community reaches "a tipping
point" for better or for ill? What is the action or incident or series of
changes that drive people (and businesses) away, or that bring them
back? What incites a stampede to get out, and what, in turn, becomes the
lure for people to return? What critical mass is necessary before someone
says, "I'd like to live there," instead of, "I'm moving out"?

What is the role of politics in all of this? Planners and academic researchers spend countless hours measuring densities and property values,
commuting patterns and vehicle miles traveled, increases in building permits and the effects of zoning policies. But politics—who is in power, who
that person appoints to key positions, and what motivates political leaders—
has always played a critical role in how these complex land use and planning issues are decided and implemented.

The Maryland experiment was rooted in one governor's personality
and experiences, channeled by the rough-and-tumble politics of the time,
buffeted by the often unbending intransigence of county governments,
and boosted by clever marketing and the aura of national celebrity.

This book does not pretend to offer a comprehensive analysis of the
performance of the Maryland Smart Growth program. Other more capable researchers are hard at work on such assessments. There are, nevertheless, important lessons for decision makers at all levels of
government that can be gleaned from the political approach Parris N.
Glendening and his staff took to the task of dealing with the multifac-
eted, stubbornly resistant, and politically explosive set of issues many
Americans now refer to collectively as "Smart Growth."

## 1.  Lead It

*There is absolutely no substitute for having strong leadership from the top.*

Maryland's Smart Growth program would not have happened without the strong, determined, relentless leadership of Parris Glendening.
It is fair to dissect the program that the Glendening administration put
in place as to whether it was effective or accomplished what it set out to
achieve. But there is no question that none of it would have happened
without the chief executive of state government leading the way.

## 2. Limit It

*Know your political parameters before you start.*

At the outset, Glendening and his staff understood how far they could go within the real political world of Maryland in 1997 and did not overreach. They paid attention to the lessons of the past and knew, for example, it would be futile to try a heavy-handed approach to shift power from the counties to the state.

Given budget constraints at the time, the governor also knew the new program must not be seen as a big new spending program. That was not only a pragmatic approach, but a strategic one as well: he did not want his new land use program to come under attack as a drain on limited financial resources that potential supporters might rather see spent elsewhere.

Perhaps the most important parameter was that the new initiative was to take an incentive-based approach rather than regulatory. Regulations, Glendening believed, created more enemies than friends. Intuitively and politically, he knew an incentive-based program would have a softer landing in the legislature and with the public at large. In retrospect, it was the incentive-based nature of the Maryland program that seemed to attract so much attention from outside the state.

Finally, the Maryland program would be unabashedly pro-growth. It would not be "no growth" or "slow growth." The state's intention was to support well-planned growth, especially in areas already supported by infrastructure and services. Because the program embraced growth, home builders, developers, and even the property rights advocates who might otherwise have opposed the Smart Growth initiative were neutralized. They wanted to know the new rules, of course, and they wanted those rules to be fairly and consistently applied. But as long as the state was not trying to stop growth, they were willing let the program unfold.

## 3. Measure It

*Set goals so you know where you are headed and whether you are getting there.*

At the time the Smart Growth initiative was being developed, the governor and his staff were thoroughly convinced that Maryland's development trends were detrimental to the state's long-term interests. Despite that, the state never made any attempt to set specific goals or benchmarks for what it intended to achieve through the Smart Growth initiative. It, therefore, did not have—and still does not have—any way of measuring if the program was succeeding.

In pushing Smart Growth to passage, the state relied on a wealth of statistics, mostly produced by the Office of Planning, detailing suburban household migration, lot size growth, the effects of abandonment in

Baltimore City, the rise in vehicle miles traveled, and so on. Yet, those who put the Smart Growth initiative together never asked how the state would know if the Smart Growth initiative was successful. There were no benchmarks, no goals, no plans for measuring change.

This shortcoming can be explained, in part, by the fact that the Smart Growth staff faced more fundamental concerns, not the least of which was whether they could muster the majorities needed to enact the proposal. But it is certainly true that without knowing where the program was headed, it was impossible for anyone to know later whether it was reaching its destination. This became something of a political embarrassment when state officials were later pressed to demonstrate the program's success but had little beyond anecdotal examples to offer. Not only could such an evaluation have led to policy improvement, it also could have produced the political ammunition needed to press for more fundamental change. In hindsight, skipping this important step was a mistake.

## 4.  Envision It

*Envision your future and let that vision guide your land use decisions.*

Maryland's Smart Growth initiative—and, for that matter, the growth management efforts of previous years—was never based on any regional or statewide visioning exercise that might have determined what the public thought their state or region should look like in the future. The governor's staff did a commendable job reaching out to several hundred private sector, nonprofit, and governmental organizations to solicit ideas as the Smart Growth initiative was being formulated. But most of that feedback was specific to individual programs or problems. The public at large was never engaged.

By failing to develop a mechanism through which citizens from different parts of the state could develop their own vision for how "smart growth" should be locally defined, the program created opponents where supporters could have been found. Without broader public involvement at the beginning, political support from the public had to be developed after the fact.

## 5.  Name It

*Pick a short, catchy name that summarizes what you are trying to achieve.*

One of the smartest decisions the Glendening administration made was to brand its land use initiative with the name "Smart Growth." While there is abundant evidence that this phrase was not first coined in Maryland, there is little doubt that the Maryland program succeeded in popularizing it. Those two words summarized a broad set of issues with a phrase catchy enough to grab people's attention and difficult for anyone to oppose. Who would want to be against "Smart Growth"? The phrase also helped mollify the suspicious pro-growth crowd, assuring them the state was not trying to stop or slow growth, but rather to support it as long as it was "smart."

Almost as soon as the initiative was named, it became obvious that those who opposed "Smart Growth" must inevitably favor "dumb growth." Over time, of course, this became an irritant, especially among those local elected officials and planners who suddenly found that the work they had been doing so proudly for years denigrated and dismissed as "dumb growth." From a political standpoint, those two words conveyed the fundamental belief that the patterns of growth experienced in the United States for the past half-century have not been in the collective best interest of citizens and should be improved. Everyone could be smarter about it.

Today, the phrase "Smart Growth" works in some settings, but not in others. To some, it carries the partisan baggage of Parris Glendening and Al Gore. Some equate it—erroneously—with one-size-fits-all, top-down regulatory approaches that are usually unpopular with the public. To others, it is simply insulting. As a result, dozens of other names have been tried as substitutes: "Livable Communities," "Balanced Growth," "Quality Growth," "Sustainable Growth," "Priority Places," and so on. But even when these new names are used, the press and public often still refer to these programs under the old banner, "Smart Growth."

An intangible and unmeasurable effect of the spread of the phrase "Smart Growth" is the degree to which it has empowered everyday citizens to talk about issues that once seemed to be the exclusive language of builders, planners, and traffic engineers. It has enabled the public to see that where and how development occurs is directly connected to their quality of life and prompts them to ask the question: Are we being smart about it? To build political support, the public has to be able to talk about the issue.

## 6. Sell It

*To be successful, elected leaders must wrap their substantive land use reforms within an aggressive communications and marketing strategy.*

No matter how good your ideas, how clever your strategies, how creative your financing proposals, or how important your program is to the future of your jurisdiction's quality of life, it is not likely to succeed unless it is wrapped within a carefully planned, comprehensive communications strategy. Changing growth patterns is hard work, politically risky, often extremely unpopular with one or more important groups in a community, so you need to articulate why it is necessary to act now. Moreover, it is important to explain why the current system is not working, what will be the impact if the system is not changed, and why it is in the jurisdiction's collective interest to develop smarter, more sustainable growth patterns.

This communications effort will make various government agencies feel as if they are pulling together in the same direction; and will help the public understand and accept the changes that will be necessary if Smart Growth is to really change development patterns. But to be successful, the governor (or highest political leader of the jurisdiction that is pushing for change) must agree to be the principal spokesman and must approach the task as if it were a campaign.

## 7. Share It

*Share your ideas early with those interested in or affected by the proposal.*

Another way Glendening and his staff helped sell their ideas was by alerting stakeholders early in the process of the state's intentions and inviting their input. Surprise is rarely an advantage when trying to pass legislation. Surprise irritates lawmakers and makes the interests affected by legislation suspicious and distrustful. It is difficult to muster a majority under such circumstances. Announcing legislative plans too early, however, can short-circuit the best of proposals by giving potential opponents too much time to organize an attack.

Maryland's Smart Growth program was successfully enacted, in part, because by the time the initiative was introduced, every potential stakeholder knew a proposal was coming and had been given an opportunity to offer ideas. The governor was careful not to prejudge what would be in that legislation and invited interested parties to offer suggestions.

The feedback from the groups informed the choices made by the governor and his staff. They could easily see which ideas were clearly off the table, and which ones seemed to have general support. The outreach effort may not have nailed down converts, but at least it had a calming effect.

## 8. Teach It

*Changing the culture requires educating the next generation.*

Glendening and his staff believed from the outset that all the rules and incentives the state could muster would have little effect if the general mindset toward how our land is used did not change. The governor concluded early on that it would require a change in thinking to make Smart Growth successful. He called for a "Smart Growth ethos" that he compared with the spirit of the Chesapeake Bay Foundation's "Save the Bay" effort.

That kind of change takes time—maybe a generation or more. With that in mind, his staff tried to get young people to think about and discuss Smart Growth issues so they would better understand the choices they will face when they became adults. The state held four day-long Governors' Youth Environmental Summits, each attended by seven hundred to eight hundred high school students and their teachers, and each focusing on transportation, bay restoration, or other issues that are linked to or affected by development patterns.

The staff later developed a series of Smart Growth lesson plans for middle and high school teachers to use in their classrooms. With the help of a grant from a nonprofit foundation, staff offered training sessions so teachers could learn how to use the lesson plans in their classrooms.

To get young people to envision what their state would look like in the future, the state also sponsored an art and photo contest for which student participants were asked to draw, paint or photograph "The Maryland You Want." The best entries were put on display in the Maryland State House.

Working with a subsidiary of the National Geographic Society, the state's Smart Growth staff also developed a helpful student learning tool: a Maryland Smart Growth map that on one side showed the trends that led to the Smart Growth initiative and, on the other, showed the Smart Growth response.

Together, these activities acknowledged that it will take time— maybe a generation or more—to change the culture of how Marylanders view the use of their land.

## 9. Advocate It

*Encourage a "community up" approach to balance "leadership from the top."*

Just as the Smart Growth program was about to be unveiled before the Maryland General Assembly, the Maryland Office of Planning quietly provided a small grant that helped start a nonprofit Smart Growth advocacy group called 1000 Friends of Maryland.

Modeled after "1000 Friends" groups in other states and composed of environmentalists, developers, architects, planners, and others, this outside organization became a vocal proponent for smarter growth and a political force that could push not only state legislators and local government officials to do more, but the governor's office as well.

## 10. Praise It

*Give awards and seek awards.*

Even in its earliest days, Maryland's Smart Growth initiative was fortunate to receive numerous awards and recognition from outside organizations. Each time this happened, the importance of what the state was doing was emphasized. Outside recognition served as confirmation that the approach was valuable. Praise begat acceptance.

Similarly, the Smart Growth staff steadily built support and momentum for the program by giving awards. The annual "Smart Growth Awards" highlighted smart developments, regional cooperation, new transit initiatives,

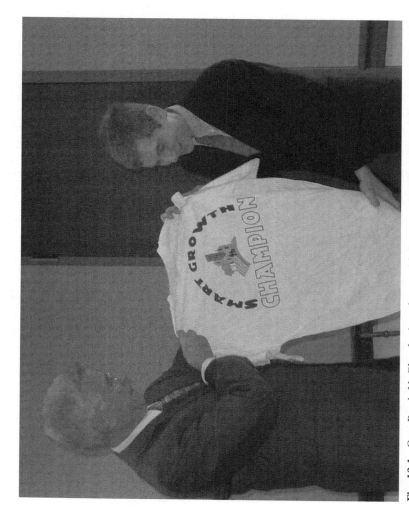

**Fig. 13.1.** Gov. Parris N. Glendening always said that to make Smart Growth work, "You have to change the culture." Here he is with a young "Smart Growth Champion," Baltimore student Ben Hyman, who donated his own money to the Smart Growth cause.

innovative builders, and individual local government leaders who were willing to take a political risk by promoting smarter growth. Local "Smart Growth Champions" were singled out each month on the Office of Smart Growth Web site.

Such praise—whether coming to the state or from the state—helped prove to the public and doubting legislators that the state was on the right course.

## 11. Blend It

*Insist on cross-departmental cooperation.*

By its nature, Smart Growth represents a cross-disciplinary set of issues. It cannot be successfully implemented if the program is housed in or the responsibility of a single agency. The staff workgroup that put Maryland's Smart Growth initiative together represented all the major state agencies: planning, environment, natural resources, economic development, general services, budget and management, housing and community development. This working group became the template for cross-departmental cooperation through which the program would later be administered.

But making this happen was neither easy nor automatic. Department chiefs have their own agendas and ideas, their own constituencies and their own set of pressures. They must sort through the scores of issues a governor may champion in any given year to determine the ones in which the governor is truly interested. Glendening not only had to sell the Smart Growth concept to the General Assembly and the public, but also to members of his own cabinet.

He did this by creating a Smart Growth Sub-Cabinet, first by executive order and later in state law. But that fact did not, by itself, cause cabinet secretaries to work together. That took the insistence of the governor: leadership from the top.

## 12. Link It

*Develop an "inside/outside" strategy.*

Another element that propelled Maryland's Smart Growth initiative to passage in 1997 and to notoriety in the years that followed was its intertwined urban-rural strategy. By linking urban redevelopment with rural land preservation efforts, Glendening created a broad-based political coalition that was difficult to defeat. This inside/outside strategy provided both substantive and political benefits.

Substantively, it acknowledged that until something was done to make older towns and cities places where people wanted to live, the outward migration would continue. At the same time, it recognized that success in the older towns and cities would be slow in coming and pressure would continue to build on rural areas. Politically, this enabled the governor to build a broad, strong coalition of urban, suburban, and rural legislators who may have preferred to support one part of the program more than another, but who nonetheless were convinced to support the entire program and—together—provided enough votes to get it passed. Politically, there was something in it for everyone.

## 13.  Fund It

*To make an incentive-based initiative work, you have to fund it.*

As the Maryland program was coming together in 1996, the central question became: If the state could not control the land use decisions of local government, then what could it control? The answer was remarkably obvious: it could control where it spent state money. Moreover, Glendening was convinced that it mattered to builders, developers, and local governments where the state invested its resources—that such investments could make a project happen and the absence of state funds could grind a project to a halt.

State government in Maryland had never before restricted the use of its financial resources in this way. It didn't stop growth; it rewarded "smart" growth. It didn't cost the state more; it enabled the state to spend what it already was spending more efficiently. It represented a better, more thoughtful use of resources. It required all counties to use the same basic framework for identifying growth and preservation areas. And, it positioned the state so that it set the example that local governments might follow.

Having said this, a fundamental problem of the Maryland program was that the financial incentives the state offered were never sufficient to prompt the kind of changes the administration hoped to achieve. A study ten years after the Smart Growth program was enacted* showed that only about 5 percent of the overall state budget each year is targeted for spending on projects inside PFAs and most of that money consists of spending on transportation projects. Researchers suggested that it may be because such a relatively small proportion of the state budget is restricted to projects within designated growth areas that PFAs do not seem to be constraining growth or curbing sprawl development as envisioned when the Smart Growth program was created. The state, of course, had other budgetary priorities that had to be met. But in many instances, the state was

---

*Gerrit-Jan Knaap and Rebecca Lewis, *State Agency Spending Under Maryland's Smart Growth Areas Act: Who's Tracking, Who's Spending, How Much, and Where?*, National Center for Smart Growth Research and Education, University of Maryland, September 30, 2007.

not able to offer enough money to convince builders, developers, or local governments to do things differently. In many more instances, a subsidy from the state was never sought in the first place and therefore had no bearing on the ultimate development decision.

More importantly, the incentives offered under the Smart Growth law mostly affected new development projects for which state financial assistance was considered necessary. If neither a project's developer nor the local government wanted or sought state financial assistance, a project was essentially unaffected by the Smart Growth law. Moreover, local governments retained the authority to approve projects regardless of whether they were within the Priority Funding Areas designated under the Smart Growth law.

The second serious problem with an incentive-based approach is that it is always subject to changing political priorities and economic cycles. If a new administration at the state level decides to appropriate funds for different purposes—as happened under Governor Ehrlich—the Smart Growth programs lose their punch. If the economy declines or the state refuses to raise sufficient revenues to cover its costs, then programs that might otherwise be used as incentives are cut.

The obvious political lesson is that an incentive-based program without sufficient funds for incentives does not hold much promise for creating change. To be effective, Maryland's Smart Growth program needed more money for incentives, not less.

## 14. Strengthen It

*If the policies you impose are not strong enough, strengthen them.*

The structure and ground rules for the basic planning block of Maryland's Smart Growth initiatives, the Priority Funding Areas, ultimately proved to be too weak and porous to slow sprawl, much less stop it. As a method of focusing where the state spent its money on growth, PFAs were fine; but when judged as a sprawl containment measure, they were a failure.

Maryland's PFAs were never set up to be an Oregon-style Urban Growth Boundary, which separates where growth is allowed and where it is not. Even the Urban Rural Demarcation Line used by planners in Baltimore County since 1967 provides stronger separation of growth and no-growth areas than do the PFAs under the state's Smart Growth program.

The hard reality is that this central Smart Growth concept does not prevent growth outside of PFA boundaries: It only prevents the use of state funds to assist projects that are outside of PFAs. If a project does not require or seek state financial assistance and is otherwise approved by a local government, the PFA designation has no bearing on the project or its location.

There is anecdotal evidence that the mere creation of PFAs and the subsequent public attention that has been directed to decisions on whether new projects are to be located inside or outside PFA boundaries has had a salutary effect on local government decisions. And, the PFA boundaries have provided a framework with which to judge local government development decisions. The fact remains, however, that the universe of projects affected by the PFA designation has been relatively small.

With the passage of time, it may now be politically possible to revisit the topic of Priority Funding Areas and develop ways that this important Smart Growth tool can be strengthened.

## 15. Change It

*Demonstrate a willingness to depart from "business as usual."*

Smart Growth meant nothing, Glendening thought, if state agencies continued "business as usual." To prove its political effectiveness, he insisted that department secretaries review their budgets and projects to identify funding or approaches that must change in order to be consistent with Smart Growth policy.

As a result, the governor and his cabinet secretaries demonstrated a willingness to make tough decisions to do things differently than they were done in the past. They cancelled highway bypass projects; they threatened counties that had up-zoned farmland with the loss of farmland preservation funds; and the state began intervening in local government land use decisions, often supporting Smart Growth projects that might otherwise die in the face of local opposition.

Consistent with the governor's executive order, the state insisted that new state facilities or offices be located in downtown areas of towns and cities rather than on the outskirts of town, which had become the norm for courthouses, motor vehicle offices, or other state offices or facilities. State agencies also began to use funds in novel new ways: transportation funds that in the past might have been used to expand suburban roadway capacity were instead used to improve older state roads that ran through the heart of older small towns and cities. In many cases, these roads had not been upgraded in decades. State funds for public school construction and renovation were also targeted to older schools in older areas (by definition, within Priority Funding Areas) rather than mostly for new schools in suburban and rural locations.

It took political courage each time the state took one of these actions, but after awhile it seemed more surprising when state government actions *did not* support the broader Smart Growth goals.

## 16.  Augment It

*Continuously add to and improve the initiative.*

One concept that contributed to the momentum the Smart Growth program developed during the Glendening years was that neither the governor nor his staff ever viewed the 1997 legislation as an end in itself. Rather, they saw it as a start. They knew that to achieve real change, they had to augment the original initiative by layering on new proposals every year.

When, for example, it became obvious that the state's historic preservation tax credit was becoming one of the most effective incentives for redevelopment, the administration and the General Assembly steadily increased the size of the tax credit available to participating developers.

When local codes were identified as a barrier to Smart Growth, Glendening held a "Smart Codes" conference and followed it with a revision of the state's building rehabilitation code and the drafting of model codes that local governments were encouraged to adopt.

When some revitalization efforts stalled because there was no program designed for certain costs, such as demolition of derelict buildings, the administration created a competitive "Community Legacy" program to meet needs not covered by some other categorical program.

The goal was to keep the pressure on; to always have something ready to move to the front burner; to come back year after year with new ways to strengthen the original program. It was obvious that only so much change would be approved in any single year, so the administration looked at the distant horizon and just plugged away, year after year.

## 17.  Restructure It

*Create new political structures to achieve goals.*

Even before developing the Smart Growth initiative, Glendening convened many of his cabinet officers as a single group focused on revitalization. After the Smart Growth measures were enacted in 1997, he issued an executive order the following year establishing both the Smart Growth Sub-Cabinet and the staff level Smart Growth Coordinating Committee.

Later, deciding he still needed more oomph from his Smart Growth program, he established an Office of Smart Growth directly within the Office of the Governor. The Office of Smart Growth was expected to encourage more cooperation among departments and provide technical advice on specific development projects to builders, developers, or even local governments.

Each time the governor felt the existing political structures were not producing the results he wanted, he created new ones that he hoped would do better.

## 18.  Value It

*Target growth to areas where it already exists.*

For decades, older communities in Maryland had been neglected as state resources and attention instead were directed to new developments in the suburbs or the rural fringe. The Smart Growth initiative attempted to reverse this by placing more value on the areas that were already developed.

For Glendening, this also provided a political advantage: it split what might otherwise have been solid local government opposition to greater state involvement in land use issues. By emphasizing the importance of existing cities and towns, Glendening immediately brought the state's mayors and other municipal leaders to his side, and to the side of Smart Growth. Mayors were among Smart Growth's strongest supporters. Politically, this isolated county leaders who opposed Smart Growth.

## 19.  Unite It

*The state cannot do it alone.*

Faced with political realities, the Smart Growth initiative made very little headway in changing the paradigm of local land use control. As a result, the success of the state program largely hinged on the actions of local government officials over which the state had little or no control. If local decisions went contrary to the general goals of Smart Growth, the state had little recourse. Ultimately, it proved that the state cannot implement a Smart Growth initiative alone.

The governor could and did use his office as a "bully pulpit" to encourage local government adherence to Smart Growth principles. In his second term, he increasingly withheld state funds as a "stick" designed to force local governments into taking Smart Growth actions. Toward the end of his administration, the governor began to invoke a little-used state authority to intervene in local land use decisions as a means of steering Smart Growth projects to approval or defeating projects that were at odds with Smart Growth goals.

In the final analysis, however, the authority to decide where growth should occur remained at the local level, often guided by the same parochial political interests that created the state's sprawling development pattern in the first place.

Any effort to transfer land use authority from the local governments to the state surely would have been met with vehement opposition from the counties and would have been unlikely to pass. But without such change, there was still no governmental entity with the authority to look at the overall development picture and decide what decisions would result in the greatest good for the greatest number of people.

## 20. Institutionalize It

*Put it in the law.*

Throughout his years in office, Glendening purposely tried to institutionalize as much of the Smart Growth program as possible so it would survive after he left office. At times, the governor even sought legislative approval when none was needed.

The fight for smarter growth was to be a long-term struggle, not something accomplished in a year or two or even within a four-year term or two four-year terms. By institutionalizing as much of the program as possible, the governor sought to shelter the effort against the vicissitudes of politics.

But because the Maryland Smart Growth initiative was institutionalized almost completely at the state government level, its continuance became problematic once there was a regime change. When Maryland got a new governor in January 2003, the state's Smart Growth movement almost immediately began to falter. Veteran staff who had worked on the program since its inception and, in some cases, worked on related issues since before its inception voluntarily left state service or were asked to leave. Funds for Smart Growth programs were sharply reduced and, in some instances, eliminated.

Moreover, the philosophy of the new governor was to leave local governments alone and let them continue to make their own land use decisions without state interference, regardless of the financial or other effects those decisions might have on the state as a whole or on neighboring jurisdictions. Absent strong leadership from the state and without sufficient financial incentives to get their attention, many local governments returned to "business-as-usual."

Nevertheless, by imbedding the Smart Growth initiative in state statute, it made it harder for Glendening's successor to eliminate or completely ignore the program. That's because the statutes provided a rallying point for Smart Growth supporters, who pressed the new governor to get more fully behind the Smart Growth law. When he failed to do so, it opened a political opportunity for his opponent in the next gubernatorial election to promise that, if elected, he would "revive" Smart Growth.

## Do It All

The final political lesson is that none of this advice by itself will be enough. To succeed, elected leaders probably have to do it all. And more.

# Appendix

## Milestones in Maryland Land Use Planning

1904    Zoning in Maryland begins with a grant of authority by the General Assembly to Baltimore to limit the height of buildings within certain designated areas; similar authority was subsequently granted to other cities.

1924    Cities of Cumberland and Takoma Park granted authority to establish zoning commissions and boards of adjustments for the purpose of securing more orderly development and better utilization of city property.

1927    General Assembly enacts a general zoning enabling act authorizing cities of ten thousand or more to zone; it also established the Maryland-Washington Metropolitan District under the control of the Maryland-National Capital Park & Planning Commission.

1933    General Assembly enacts the Planning Enabling Act, which confers planning and zoning authority upon any municipality; the term *municipality* is defined as "counties, cities or other incorporated areas."

1967    Maryland Environmental Trust established to conserve, improve, stimulate, and perpetuate the aesthetic, natural, scenic, and cultural aspects of the Maryland environment.

1969    Program Open Space (parkland acquisition) established.

1973    Shore Erosion Control Program provides loans and grants to prevent shore erosion of the Chesapeake Bay and its tributaries.

1974    Maryland Planning Act enacted, giving the state authority to intervene in local land use decisions and authorizing the Maryland Department of Planning to create a state development plan.

1977    Maryland Agricultural Land Preservation Program created to preserve agricultural land and woodland in Maryland.

1982    Stormwater Management Act requires on-site treatment of stormwater on new development sites to prevent nonpoint source pollution.

1982    First comprehensive state policies for physical and economic development put into effect by gubernatorial executive order, establishing six principles to guide state investments and actions, among them: enhance the viability of existing communities and urban areas; and protect productive agricultural land and assure the conservation and wise balanced use of natural resources.

1983    Multistate Chesapeake Bay agreement signed by Virginia, Maryland, Pennsylvania, District of Columbia, and U.S. EPA. The agreement recognizes that population growth and its associated development patterns are major causes of environmental degradation.

1984    Chesapeake Bay Critical Areas Program establishes restrictions on land use activities within a 1,000-foot area along the shoreline of the Chesapeake Bay and its tidal tributaries.

1988    "Year 2020 Panel," created as a result of the regional Chesapeake Bay agreement, directed to produce a report on growth management regulations, environmental programs and infrastructure requirements necessary to protect the bay while still accommodating projected population growth in the bay region through 2020.

1989    State authorizes protection of nontidal wetlands.

1992    Economic Growth, Resource Protection and Planning Act enacted, establishing seven "visions" for development in Maryland and statewide growth management policies and mandates.

1992    Forest Conservation Act adopted to protect Maryland forests.

1997    Brownfields cleanup and redevelopment legislation enacted.

1997    Smart Growth initiative (Smart Growth Areas Act, Rural Legacy Program, Job Creation Tax Credit, Live Near Your Work program) enacted.

2000    "Smart Codes" legislation to establish new statewide rehabilitation building code and create model infill and mixed-use development codes.

2000    National Center for Smart Growth Research and Education created at the University of Maryland.

2001    Community Legacy Program enacted to provide flexible funding to support local revitalization projects.

2001    Maryland Office of Smart Growth established as a direct arm of the governor's office with oversight responsibility for Smart Growth activities in all state agencies.

2003    Office of Smart Growth transferred to Department of Planning; Priority Places program established by gubernatorial executive order and Maryland Department of Planning put in charge of Smart Growth effort.

2003    Development Capacity Task Force develops protocol for Maryland counties and municipalities to determine their future development capacity.

2004    General Assembly rejects gubernatorial effort to abolish the Office of Smart Growth; "Flush Tax" enacted by the General Assembly.

2006    General Assembly adds two new planning elements required in local government comprehensive plans: a municipal growth element and a water resources element, which addresses drinking water supply and wastewater and stormwater management.

# Notes

## Chapter 1.  Room 217

1.  Keith Schneider, "Ending Sprawl Isn't About Stopping All Development," *Detroit Free Press*, February 22, 1998.

2.  John M. DeGrove, *Planning Policy and Politics: Smart Growth and the States* (Cambridge, Mass.: Lincoln Institute of Land Policy, 2005), 2–3.

3.  Robert Timberg, "Money Becomes Big Issue in Governor's Race," *Baltimore Sun*, October 23, 1994.

4.  State-of-the-State address by Governor Marvin Mandel, *Journal of Proceedings of the Senate*, Jan. 17, 1973, 228.

5.  Critical Areas Law, Section 8-1807 of the Natural Resources Article, Annotated Code of Maryland.

6.  James R. Cohen, "Maryland's 'Smart Growth': Using Incentives to Combat Sprawl," in G. Squires (ed.), *Urban Sprawl: Causes, Consequences, and Policy Responses* (Washington, D.C.: Urban Institute Press, 2002).

7.  See:      http://www.chesapeakebay.net/pubs/1983ChesapeakeBay Agreement.pdf.

8.  The 2020 Commission, *Population Growth and Development in the Chesapeake Bay Watershed to the Year 2020*, The Report of the Year 2020 Panel of to the Chesapeake Bay Executive Council. Annapolis, Md.: Chesapeake Bay Program, December 1988.

9.  Author interview with Ronald M. Kreitner, December 20, 2004.

10.  Author interview with John R. Griffin, October 25, 2004.

11.  Ibid.

12.  Cohen, "Maryland's 'Smart Growth.'"

13.  Ibid.

14.  Author interview with Ronald M. Kreitner, December 20, 2004.

15.  Ibid.

16.  *Making a Great State Greater*, Maryland Commission on State Taxes and Tax Structure, R. Robert Linowes Chairman, December 1990.

17.  The Economic Growth, Resource Protection and Planning Act of 1992, Md. Code Ann., State Fin. & Proc. Sect. 5-7A-02 (2000).

18. *Managing Maryland's Growth: What You Need to Know about Smart Growth and Neighborhood Conservation,* Maryland Office of Planning, Publication #97-05, May 1997, 16.

19. *Overview of Planning Programs,* Maryland Department of Planning and Maryland Department of the Environment, 2006, 5, http://www.mdp.state.md.us/pdf/toolboxpub.pdf.

20. Author interview with Ronald M. Kreitner, December 20, 2004.

21. Author notes from internal meeting with gubernatorial aides Ron Young, Patricia Payne, Ronald M. Kreitner, Lynda Fox, Victor Hoskins, and Tom Osborne, March 13, 1996.

22. Cabinet Revitalization and Directed Growth Strategy Meeting agenda, area map, participation list, and Office of Planning presentation, December 15, 1995.

23. Cabinet Revitalization and Directed Growth Strategy Meeting of December 15, 1995, minutes (undated).

## Chapter 2. Brownfields, Chapman's Landing, and the Chestertown Wal-Mart

1. Author interview with John R. Griffin, October 25, 2004.

2. Author notes from internal meeting with Glendening and staff, January 1996.

3. Author notes from internal meeting with Glendening and staff, Jan. 11, 1996.

4. Author interview with John R. Griffin , October 25, 2004.

5. Ibid.

6. Ibid.

7. Ibid.

8. Author notes from internal meeting with Glendening and staff, February 22, 1996.

9. Author's notes from internal meeting with Glendening, Dru Schmidt-Perkins of Clean Water Action, Joy Oakes of the Sierra Club, George Maurer of the Chesapeake Bay Foundation, and Jane Nishida of the Maryland Department of Environment.

10. Letter to Colonel Randall R. Inouyo, U.S. Army Corps of Engineers, from Virginia state Senator Joseph V. Gartlan Jr., dated June 5, 1997; and, letter to Martin Lancaster, Assistant Secretary of the Army (Civil Works), from U.S. Senator Charles S. Robb and U.S. Rep. James P. Moran, dated June 26, 1997.

11. David Payne, "Study Shows Water Supply OK to 2020," *Maryland Independent,* Waldorf, Md., April 25, 1997.

12. Confidential memo from John W. Frece to Eleanor Carey and Jane Nishida, re Chapman's Landing Briefing on July 2, 1997, dated June 26, 1997.

13. Ibid.

14. Todd Shields and Peter S. Goodman, "Md. To Buy, Preserve Tract in Charles," *Washington Post,* August 21, 1998.

15. Author interview with John R. Griffin, October 25, 2004.

16. A History of Chestertown, http://www.chestertown.com/C-300/history.htm.

17. Author's notes from internal meeting with Glendening, Ronald M. Kreitner, and Eugene Lynch, March 19, 1996.

18. Ibid.

# Chapter 3. "Tell Them, 'The Governor Is Very Serious.'"

1. Author notes from internal meeting with Glendening and staff, April 2, 1996.

2. Author notes from internal meeting with Glendening, Senators Brian Frosh, Michael Collins, and Clarence Blount, Delegates John Hurson, Anita Stup, and Ronald Guns, and other Glendening staff, April 8, 1996.

3. Ibid.

4. Author notes from internal meeting of the "Directed Growth" staff, April 9, 1996.

5. Draft Executive Order 01.01.1996, Cabinet Council on Directed Growth, Revitalization, and Neighborhood Conservation, circulated to Glendening staff by memo from chief legislative officer Steven B. Larsen on April 15, 1996.

6. Author's notes from internal meeting with Glendening and "Directed Growth" workgroup, April 18, 1996.

7. Ibid.

8. Ibid.

9. Ibid.

10. Ibid.

11. Ibid.

12. Author's notes from internal meeting with Glendening and "Directed Growth" workgroup, May 3, 1996.

13. Ibid.

14. Ibid.

15. Author's notes of internal meeting with Will Baker, president of the Chesapeake Bay Foundation, May 14, 1996.

16. Ibid.

17. Ibid.

18. Developed by Timothy Foresman (UMBC) and Penny Masuoka (NASA/Goddard Space Flight Center Scientific Visualization Studio) based on data from 1792 to 1992, the project was completed on April 15, 1996. It can be found at: http://svs.gsfc.nasa.gov/vis/a000000/a000000/a000099/.

19. Author's notes of internal meeting with Kreitner and other members of the "Directed Growth" workgroup, June 18, 1996.

20. "Sprawling 'Burbs Next Battlefront?" *Baltimore Business Journal,* June 18, 1996.

21. Author notes from internal meetings with Glendening and staff on June 6 and June 18, 1996.

22. "Where Do We Grow from Here?" remarks by Governor Parris N. Glendening, Maryland Municipal League, June 24, 1996.

23. Author interview with Stuart Meck, October 27, 2004.

24. Author interview with Harriet Tregoning, November 5, 2004.

25. Author interview with Ronald M. Kreitner, December 20, 2004.
26. Ibid.
27. Ibid.
28. Ibid.
29. Ibid.
30. Ibid.
31. Author interview with Steven B. Larsen, December 20, 2004.
32. Ibid.
33. "Where Do We Grow from Here?"
34. Ibid.
35. Parris N. Glendening, "A State Agenda to Stop Sprawl," *Baltimore Sun*, June 26, 1996.
36. Ibid.

## Chapter 4. The Initiative Begins to Take Place

1. "Where Do We Grow from Here?" remarks by Governor Parris N. Glendening, Maryland Municipal League, June 24, 1996.
2. Ibid.
3. "Neighborhood Conservation, Smart Growth: We Asked, You Proposed, Now We Need Your Recommendations," Maryland Office of Planning, Summer 1996.
4. Author's notes from internal meeting with James T. Brady and other workgroup staff, September 5, 1996.
5. Author's notes from internal meeting of workgroup, September 10, 1996.

## Chapter 5. The Inside/Outside Strategy

1. Author interview with John R. Griffin, October 25, 2004.
2. The Financial and Legal Subcommittee included: Kevin Quinn (H. C. Wainwright & Co.), Daniel O'Connell (Evergreen Financial Advisors), Hans Mayer (MEDCO), Fred Puddester (Dept. of Budget and Fiscal Planning), Tom Filbert (OAG /MDA), Jodi O'Day (OAG/DNR), John Griffin (DNR), Lewis Riley (MDA), Ron Kreitner (OP), and was staffed by Doug Wilson, Paul Scheidt (MDA), and Grant Dehart (DNR).
3. Bond Financing for Land Conservation, a report for J. Charles Fox and Michael J. Nelson, Maryland Department of Natural Resources, August 2002, by H. Grant Dehart, Capital Grants and Loan Administration, Department of Natural Resources.
4. Author interview with H. Grant Dehart, November 11, 2004.
5. Author interview with John R. Griffin, October 25, 2004.
6. Confidential letter from John R. Griffin to Parris N. Glendening dated September 11, 1996.
7. Ibid.
8. Ibid.
9. Ibid.

10. Ibid.

11. Ibid.

12. Ibid.

13. Author interview with John R. Griffin, October 25, 2004.

14. Confidential letter from John R. Griffin to Parris N. Glendening dated September 11, 1996.

15. Ibid.

16. Author interview with H. Grant Dehart, November 11, 2004.

## Chapter 6.  "The Most Important Thing in the Whole Administration"

1. Memorandum entitled "Sustainable Development Strategy," from Sandy Hillyer to John Frece, September 11, 1996.

2. Ibid.

3. Ibid.

4. Ibid.

5. Author notes from Smart Growth staff retreat, Wye Island, September 27, 1996.

6. Ibid.

7. Ibid.

8. Author's notes from internal meeting with Glendening and staff, October 4, 1996.

9. Ibid.

10. Ibid.

11. Author notes of two internal meetings with Glendening and staff on October 16, 1996.

12. Ibid.

13. Ibid.

14. Ibid.

15. Ibid.

16. Ibid.

17. Ibid.

18. Author's notes from internal meeting with staff on October 17, 1996.

19. Author's notes from internal meeting with staff on October 23, 1996.

20. Ibid.

21. Author interview with Ronald M. Kreitner, December 20, 2004.

22. Author's notes from meeting with Karen Lewand and Al Barry, October 29, 1996.

23. Ibid.

24. Author's notes from meeting with environmental leaders in Government House, November 6, 1996.

25. Ibid.

26. Ibid.

27. Ibid.

28. Ibid.

29. Author interview with John R. Griffin, October 25, 2004.
30. Author's notes from meeting with environmental leaders in Government House, November 6, 1996.
31. Ibid.

## Chapter 7. Opposition Solidifies

1. Author's notes from internal meeting with Glendening and staff, November 8, 1996.
2. Ibid.
3. Ibid.
4. Author interview with H. Grant Dehart, November 11, 2004.
5. Senate Bill 226 and House Bill 491, 1997 session of the Maryland General Assembly.
6. Author's notes from internal meeting with Glendening and staff, November 8, 1996.
7. Author's notes from internal meeting with James T. Brady and other members of the workgroup, November 26, 1996.
8. Ibid.
9. Ibid.
10. Ibid.
11. Author's notes from internal meeting with workgroup, November 19, 1996.
12. Author interview with Steven B. Larsen, December 20, 2004.
13. Author notes from internal meeting with Al Barry, Karen Lewand, Steven B. Larsen, Ronald N. Kreitner, and Dianna Rossborough, late November or early December 1996.
14. Author notes from cabinet meeting, December 5, 1996.
15. Author notes on meeting at which state legislators were briefed on the Smart Growth initiative, December 17, 1996.
16. Ibid.
17. Ibid.
18. Ibid.
19. Ibid.
20. Ibid.
21. Ibid.
22. Ibid.

## Chapter 8. The General Assembly Battle

1. Author's notes from Glendening's private meeting with the *Baltimore Sun* editorial board, January 3, 1997.
2. Ibid.
3. Timothy Wheeler, "Sprawl Burdens Taxpayers, Governor Warns," *Baltimore Sun,* January 12, 1997.
4. Senate Bill 389 of the 1997 session of the Maryland General Assembly.
5. Senate Bill 388 and House Bill 507 of the 1997 session of the Maryland General Assembly.

6. House Bill 409 of the 1997 session of the Maryland General Assembly.

7. Senate Bill 229 and House Bill 499 of the 1997 session of the Maryland General Assembly.

8. Senate Bill 226 and House Bill 491 of the 1997 session of the Maryland General Assembly.

9. Chapters 1 and 2, Acts of 1997.

10. Ibid.

11. Timothy B. Wheeler, "Farms' Right to Smell Draws Complaints: Neighbors Opposed to Glendening's Plan to Strengthen Law," *Baltimore Sun*, March 25, 1997.

12. Author interview with Ronald M. Kreitner, December 20, 2004.

13. Author interview with Steven B. Larsen, December 20, 2004.

14. Author interview with Ronald M. Kreitner, December 20, 2004.

15. Ibid.

16. Ibid.

17. Author interview with H. Grant Dehart, November 11, 2004.

18. Ibid.

19. Author interview with Steven B. Larsen, December 20, 2004.

20. Author interview with Ronald M. Kreitner, December 20, 2004.

21. Ibid.

22. Ibid.

23. Author notes from internal meeting with staff on January 22, 1997.

24. Author interview with former Maryland Department of Planning chief planner, James T. Noonan, January 25, 2007.

25. Author interview with Ronald M. Kreitner, December 20, 2004.

26. Senate Bill 389, Chapter 759, Acts of 1997, page 7, (F), lines 30–34.

27. Senate Bill 389, Chapter 759, Acts of 1997, page 7, (E), lines 26–29.

28. Author interview with Ronald M. Kreitner, December 20, 2004.

29. Author interview with Steven B. Larsen, December 20, 2004.

30. Terry M. Neal, "Maryland Senate Passes Measure to Limit Suburban Sprawl; Glendening's Plan Faces Hurdle in House," *Washington Post*, March 28, 1997.

31. Ibid.

32. Author interview with Ronald M. Kreitner, December 20, 2004.

33. Author interview with Steven B. Larsen, December 20, 2004.

34. Author interview with Ronald M. Kreitner, December 20, 2004.

35. Ibid.

36. Author interview with Steven B. Larsen, December 20, 2004.

37. Ibid.

38. Ibid.

39. Ibid.

40. Author interview with Ronald M. Kreitner, December 20, 2004.

41. Ibid.

42. Author interview with Steven B. Larsen, December 20, 2004.

43. Chapters 755 and 756, Acts of 1997.

44. Chapters 757 and 758, Acts of 1997.

45. Chapter 759, Acts of 1997.

46. Terry M. Neal and David Montgomery, "In Md., A Smart Growth Consensus; Legislators on the Verge of Approving Anti-Sprawl Plan, School Funds," *Washington Post*, April 5, 1997.

47. Ibid.

48. "Smart Thinking in Maryland," editorial, *Washington Post,* April 19, 1997.

49. Remarks by Governor Parris N. Glendening, Salisbury Zoological Park, Salisbury, Md., April 19, 1997.

# Chapter 9. Momentum, Implementation and Resistance

1. Charles Babington and Peter S. Goodman, "Glendening's Natural Resources; 'Green' Tilt Wins Environmental Fans, but Businesses See Red," *Washington Post,* April 7, 1998.

2. Author's notes from internal meeting with Glendening, May 30, 1997.

3. Remarks by Governor Parris N. Glendening, Smart Growth Conference, Baltimore Convention Center, June 4, 1997.

4. Neal R. Peirce, "'Smart Growth' Law Should be a Model," *Springfield Union News,* April 21, 1997.

5. Tom Brazaitis, "Smart Growth Is Smart Politics," *The Plain Dealer,* June 8, 1997.

6. Ibid.

7. House Bill 507, "Smart Growth" and Neighborhood Conservation— Rural Legacy Program, page 8, lines 5–8, 1997 session of the Maryland General Assembly, Chapter 757 and 758, Acts of 1997.

8. House Bill 507, "Smart Growth" and Neighborhood Conservation— Rural Legacy Program, page 12, lines 4–36, and page 13, lines 1–7, 1997 session of the Maryland General Assembly, Chapter 757 and 758, Acts of 1997. The Advisory Committee was appointed by the governor and comprised of members representing the Maryland Agricultural Land Preservation Foundation, Maryland Environmental Trust, the agricultural industry, a nonprofit land preservation organization, a nonprofit environmental organization, the forest industry, a representative of a county government department of parks and recreation, a business organization, a private land owner, the mineral resources industry, and an incorporated municipality.

9. Todd Shields and Peter Goodman, "Maryland to Buy, Preserve Tract in Charles," *Washington Post,* August 21, 1998.

10. Charles Babington and Peter S. Goodman, "Glendening's Natural Resources; 'Green' Tilt Wins Environmental Fans, but Businesses See Red," *Washington Post,* April 7, 1998.

11. "Not a Smart Growth Move," letter to the editor, by Ralph Bennett, Takoma Park, Md., *Washington Post,* September 4, 1998.

# Chapter 10. Second Term Freedom

1. Author's notes from cabinet meeting, December 1998.

2. Author's notes from cabinet meeting, January 1995.

3. Author interview with John D. Porcari, February 27, 2004.

4. Ibid.

5. Ibid.

6. Ibid.
7. Ibid.
8. Ibid.
9. Ibid.
10. Ibid.
11. Ibid.
12. Ibid.
13. Author notes from meeting between State Highway Administration officials and citizens of Brookeville, March 1999.
14. Author interview with John D. Porcari, February 27, 2004.
15. *Economic and Fiscal Analysis of Changes to the Historic Preservation Tax Credit Program in Maryland*, by Richard Romer and Kristen Waters, Dr. Jacqueline Rogers, School of Public Policy, and Dr. Robert Goodman, Department of Housing and Community Development, University of Maryland, March 2006, http://www.preservemd.org/html/resources.html.
16. Author notes from meeting with James R. Cohen, Tom Kennedy, Tracy Stanton, and Ron Young, Maryland Department of Planning offices, Baltimore, Fall 1999.
17. Memo to Governor Glendening from John W. Frece, National Center for Smart Growth Education and Research at the University of Maryland College Park, Supplemental Budget Request, February 28, 2000.
18. Author's notes from Smart Codes meeting, University of Maryland School of Nursing, Baltimore, May 1999.

## Chapter 11.  Clicking on All Cylinders

1. Author's note from internal meeting with Glendening, San Diego, Calif., November 23, 1999.
2. The 10 Principles of Smart Growth were originally drafted and adopted by the Smart Growth Network, a coalition of organizations brought together by the U.S. Environmental Protection Agency to share information on Smart Growth issues and activities. The 10 Principles are: (1) Create a range of housing opportunities and choices; (2) Create walkable neighborhoods; (3) Encourage community and stakeholder collaboration; (4) Foster distinctive, attractive communities with a strong sense of place; (5) Make development decisions predictable, fair, and cost effective; (6) Mix land uses; (7) Preserve open space, farmland, natural beauty, and critical environmental areas; (8) Provide a variety of transportation choices; (9) Strengthen and direct development towards existing communities; and (10) Take advantage of compact building design. See: www.smartgrowth.org/about/default/asp.
3. Tregoning served as Director of the Urban and Economic Development Division of the U.S. Environmental Protection Agency.
4. Memo to Jennifer Crawford, Deputy Chief of Staff, from John W. Frece, Special Assistant for Smart Growth, re Governor's Office of Smart Growth, December 20, 2000.
5. Ibid.
6. Ibid.

7. Ibid.

8. Author's notes of meeting with Glendening, December 27, 2000.

9. The Intermodal Surface Transportation Efficiency Act of 1991.

## Chapter 12. A Conservative's Opportunity

1. Peter Whoriskey, "Eco-Friendly Is in the Eye of Beholder; Wildlife Group's Headquarters Criticized for Suburban Sprawl," *Washington Post*, March 21, 2001.

2. "Ongoing and New Ideas for the Ehrlich Administration," a memo by John W. Frece and Julia Koster, February 17, 2003.

3. Governor's Office of Smart Growth, budget testimony by John W. Frece, Senate Budget and Taxation Committee, Public Safety, Transportation & Environment Subcommittee, February 27, 2003.

4. Ibid.

5. Ibid.

6. *Heritage Structure Rehabilitation Tax Credits: Economic and Fiscal Impacts*, prepared for Preservation Maryland by Lipman, Frizzell & Mitchell LLC, Columbia, Md., February 2002, http://www.preservemd.org/pdf/txcrstudy1.pdf.

7. Ibid.

8. Author notes from Maryland Association of Counties meeting, August 2003.

9. Executive Order 01.01.2003.33, Maryland's Priority Places Strategy, October 8, 2003.

10. Timothy B. Wheeler, "Funding Slows for Redevelopment Projects," *Baltimore Sun*, March 31, 2006.

11. *Smart Growth, Housing Markets, and Development Trends in the Baltimore-Washington Corridor*, by Gerrit-Jan Knaap, Jungyul Sohn, John W. Frece, and Elisabeth Holler, National Center for Smart Growth Research and Education, University of Maryland, prepared for the Maryland National Capital Building Industry Association and the Home Builders Association of Maryland, November 2003. http://www.smartgrowth.umd.edu/research/researchpapers-maryland.htm.

12. Final Report of the Development Capacity Task Force, July 2004, Maryland Department of Planning, page 7, Section 2.2.1.

13. 1000 Friends of Maryland, *Smart Growth: How Is Your County Doing?*, September 2001.

14. Executive Order 01.01.2004.43, Development Capacity Task Force, August 19, 2004.

15. Development Capacity Task Force Final Report, Maryland Department of Planning, http://www.mdp.state.md.us/develop_cap.htm.

16. David Nitkin, "Ehrlich Wants to End the Glendening-Era Office of Smart Growth," *Baltimore Sun*, February 4, 2004.

17. Ibid.

18. Author interview with John D. Porcari, February 27, 2004.

19. Ibid.

20. Author interview with Maryland Department of Transportation planner Nat Bottigheimer, April 22, 2004.

21.  Tom Pelton, "'Flush' Funds Enable Building; Bay Money Aids Development," *Baltimore Sun*, September 11, 2006.

22.  Ibid.

23.  *Keeping Score for the Environment: Gubernatorial Mid-Term Report Card*, League of Conservation Voters, Annapolis, Md., March 2005.

24.  Ibid.

25.  Martin O'Malley speech to the League of Conservation Voters, Annapolis, Md., September 19, 2006.

# Index